Among the Sturdy Pioneers

Among the Sturdy Pioneers

The Birth of the Cheboygan Area as a Lumbering Community, 1778-1935

Matthew J. Friday

This book is respectfully dedicated to all those who have helped me along the way, my dear family and friends, without whom none of this would have been possible.

Cover photo: timber awaiting transport via rail, Cheboygan County, about 1895.
Image © Johnson's Studio, all rights reserved

Note for Librarians: A cataloguing record for this book is available from Library and Archives
Canada at www.collectionscanada.ca/amicus/index-e.html
ISBN 1-4120-8304-4

Printed in Victoria, BC, Canada. Printed on paper with minimum 30% recycled fibre.
Trafford's print shop runs on "green energy" from solar, wind and other environmentally-friendly power sources.

Offices in Canada, USA, Ireland and UK

Book sales for North America and international:
Trafford Publishing, 6E–2333 Government St.,
Victoria, BC V8T 4P4 CANADA
phone 250 383 6864 (toll-free 1 888 232 4444)
fax 250 383 6804; email to orders@trafford.com
Book sales in Europe:
Trafford Publishing (UK) Limited, 9 Park End Street, 2nd Floor
Oxford, UK OX1 1HH UNITED KINGDOM
phone 44 (0)1865 722 113 (local rate 0845 230 9601)
facsimile 44 (0)1865 722 868; info.uk@trafford.com
Order online at:
trafford.com/06-0059

10 9 8 7 6 5 4 3 2

Don't stay cooped up in the fourth story of some tenement in the crowded cities, but come here, among the sturdy Pioneers and be a man among men.

—*Manitawauba Chronicle*, 11 February 1871

Contents

Foreword

In the summer of 1893, a young history professor named Fredrick Jackson Turner found himself at the World's Columbian Exposition in Chicago. It was a hot and humid July day, but Turner had a lot more on his mind than the heat. Rather than the summer weather, he was instead focused on a paper which he would soon present in front of his colleagues of the American Historical Association. The paper he presented, "The Significance of the Frontier in American History," is arguably one of the most important, and debated, inquires ever made into American history. The thrust of his argument was that the uniqueness of the frontier was directly responsible for developing the American nation, both in terms of its physical growth, as well as particular characteristics such as intrepidness and pioneerism its citizens possessed at both a personal and collective level. The frontier itself provided many challenges, he acknowledged, all playing a role in the development of who we are as Americans. "The peculiarity of American institutions is, the fact that they have been compelled to adapt themselves to the changes of an expanding people – to the changes involved in crossing a continent, in winning a wilderness, and in developing at each area of this progress out of the primitive economic and political conditions of the frontier into the complexity of city life." [1]

Over a hundred years later, Turner's thesis still has clout. While the exact details of the thesis frequently fall in and out of discussion among historians, no one can deny that the conditions of a newly settled area greatly affect those brave enough to settle there. The story of Cheboygan, a community on the tip of the northern Lower Peninsula of

Michigan, is itself a lesson in the history of the frontier. A *tabula rasa* far to the north, Cheboygan was settled because of the ever-increasing need for lumber. These natural resources of northern Michigan were needed as the western frontier was expanding and constantly in need of raw materials. Once the timber boom in the area began, people moved to Cheboygan in increasing numbers to be part of the action and to search out a good job, either in the forests, in the mills, or in the various other community establishments popping up almost daily. Most of the early settlers had no plans for permanent settlement, and arguably, no particular desire to be there for long either. The vast amount of timber in northern Michigan was simply a resource to be harvested, providing much needed jobs for immigrants to both Michigan specifically and the United States generally.

But Cheboygan became something more. Its prime location on the river of the same name, emptying into Lake Huron and connecting with several inland lakes, meant that the frontier lumbering community had a shot to become a more permanent settlement. The easy access to shipping not only provided a great place for moving copious amounts of product, but it also meant that the city could be an entryway into northern Michigan and more inland regions. Initially there was little desire to venture to the exceedingly remote north, but in time as lumbering faded the area's pristine lakes, fresh, clean air, and temperate climate all provided reasons for journeying north other than work.

At any rate, Cheboygan could not have become what it eventually did without lumber. The river and lakes provided the transportation, but lumber provided the men, capital, industry and commerce necessary for founding a community. Everything that happened from that point on has its foundation in Cheboygan's early lumbering days.

It truly is an amazing story. The rapidity of Cheboygan's settlement and the growth that it enjoyed for roughly five decades is a lesson not just in local or even Michigan history, but that of American history as well. The reason that so much lumber was needed was because of the expanding American nation. The taming of the West and the prosperity of the Gilded Age meant that raw material was necessary for the country's expansion. Certainly these goods were necessary for Cheboygan's growth, but more importantly they were necessary for the nation's growth as well. The fact that Cheboygan exists at all is merely a side effect of the uniquely American desire to push harder and go farther.

What resulted from this is not just one boom town, but many; nor was it a trend reserved exclusively for lumbering communities. Mining towns among mountains or villages that sprung up around oil derricks can tell a similar story. Sometimes the settlement survives after the initial boom, and sometimes it does not. Luckily for Cheboygan, the city had an excellent location on a good waterway and was in a beautiful area, so it still had merit after the lumber ran out. Communities that were not afforded natural traits such as these often died out as the economic base did as well.

Today Cheboygan still thrives in its attractive northern setting. While its population is considerably less than what it was during its peak as a lumbering community, there is still much happening in the city today. Now more service-oriented than industrial, Cheboygan is nevertheless a significant business and tourist community. None of it would have been possible, however, without the growth and progression of American westward expansion.

Fredrick Jackson Turner said in his pivotal thesis that, "Mobility of population is death to localism, and the western frontier worked irresistibly in unsettling population."[2] And so it was – Cheboygan was settled because of national expansion and the need for raw materials. Those who came to work there left their homes in the east and came to where they were needed. They abandoned their previous communities and livelihoods and sought whatever could be found further west. But when the lumber died out in Cheboygan, the story inevitably repeated itself. Localism died there just as it had in the east, and the "sturdy pioneers" again made their way further west to look for the same things that they had come to Cheboygan looking for. Indeed some people stayed, but staggering numbers left, and with them went jobs and prosperity as well. Time would heal some of these wounds, but it goes without saying that the settlement (and de-settlement) of Cheboygan was directly linked to the expansion of the American West.

In this book I have attempted to tell the beginning chapters of Cheboygan's history. I wanted to share with others what I have learned, to try to explain how and why the city was settled. Looking at contemporary sources as well as later scholarly research, I have pieced together this story and presented it here. It is a tale of exploration, settlement, boom and bust. In places I have digressed into a discussion of the lumber industry in general, because I felt it necessary to give a brief history of how logging operations were conducted. After all, without them there would have been no Cheboygan. It would not have made sense for me to mention every sawmill, every pioneer, every business and every lumber baron that ever did something in the city. My goal was to create a comprehensive, accurate, and relatively complete history of Cheboygan until the end of the lumbering era. It should be noted that there is history which unquestionably continued on after this time and continues right up until the present. However, the colorful and exciting pioneer days of the city's early history are what captivated me, and that is the history I wanted to present not merely for my own gratification, but for others to experience as well.

I wish I could personally thank everyone who helped me in this important undertaking. My first word of thanks goes to my family and friends, and all those who gave encouragement when I needed it. Without you, these words would never have been written. I also wish to thank Dr. Timothy O'Neil, Dr. David Guard, and the faculty and staff of the Department of History at Central Michigan University, with whom I have thoroughly enjoyed working. The faculty and student workers of the Clarke Historical Library also deserve my thanks, always going above and beyond bringing me out another obscure book or box of papers. Ellis Olson, a man who's wisdom I could only hope to one day attain, should be thanked not only by me but by everyone who ever reads anything about Cheboygan's history. Without him, large pieces of the story of our community would undoubtedly have been lost forever. The same can be said for Gordon Turner, whom I may not have ever met, but there is no way this work would have been possible without him. I also want to thank those who read preliminary versions of my manuscripts, provided their input, or made any kind of suggestion whatsoever. Any omissions or inaccuracies in the completed work are exclusively my own.

As a native to Cheboygan, it is my hope that this brief work will assist the reader in understanding the community that I grew up in and continue to love so much. It is my goal to help anyone who is as inquisitive as I am into not only Cheboygan, but whatever community they call home. Cheboygan's story is not unique. I hope that anyone who wants to know a little bit more about their home can understand what happened here and so reflect on their own community. Take pride in where you live, do what you can to preserve its heritage, and never stop wanting to know more. To realize who and what we are now is predicated upon a firm knowledge of what we used to be. Only with cognizance of this can we truly appreciate the present.

Matthew J. Friday
Cheboygan, Michigan
December 2005

1

The Historical Prologue

Long before the arrival of the first Europeans, Native Americans populated the region now known as Michigan. Natives had lived in the area thousands of years before the Ice Age. Sadly, that great climatic event exacted its awesome power through moving sheets of ice and destroyed most of any archeological evidence we could hope to have of them today. But afterwards, they quickly repopulated the area as the ice retreated, and began a new chapter in their, and our, history. The arrival of the white man began yet another episode in this story, and it is here, after tribal rivalries and national disputes had been put to rest that the modern story of northern Michigan began.

In the mid nineteenth century, the American "Old Northwest," of which Michigan was a part, was quickly being invaded by the white man. After admission to the Union in early 1837, the state continued to rapidly swell with settlers. Immigrants flowed in from all over, especially Canada, western New York, and from all across Europe. Most of this population stayed in the lower portion of the state, engaging in agriculture or, in fewer cases, lumbering in the Saginaw River Valley (or still more rarely in mining in the Upper Peninsula). But gradually, the lumber industry became more important to the state as westward expansion on the Great Plains took off and the demand for lumber increased. Northern Michigan was ripe with a seemingly endless supply of the highest quality wood, for use literally in building up the nation. It is a direct result of this demand that the city of Cheboygan, on the northern tip of the Lower Peninsula, developed its lumber industry. In so doing, it grew out of relative obscurity to become, at its time, one of the most important lumbering towns in the state. A significant commercial and industrial hub, Cheboygan was important not only to the local region but to the rest of the state and, on a lesser scale, the whole nation as well. Sadly however, the consequences of its growth would also be that of its decline just a few decades later. During the period 1848-1935, Cheboygan was an important lumbering and commercial community which quickly grew but gradually fell victim to that which had made it so prosperous.

*   *   *

Well before the arrival of the first white settlers the tip of the northern Lower Peninsula of Michigan was inhabited by a significant number of other residents. Prior to Cheboygan's first long-term, permanent settlers, the Chippewa and Huron Indians were making their home near the Straits of Mackinac. Native Americans probably arrived in the Western Hemisphere some 250,000 years ago (possibly as early as 400,000), and gradually made their way through what is today North America. It is impossible to know when they arrived in Michigan, considering any evidence would have been destroyed by the Ice Age 18,000 years ago. As the ice from the titanic glaciers slowly retreated, Native Americans gradually moved back into the region that now was a giant peninsula, so formed by the newly created Great Lakes, cut out and filled by the giant sheets of ice.

Over the centuries, different native groups populated the area, including the so-called Old Copper and Hopewell Indians. In time three main Indian tribes occupied what would be Michigan – the Ottawa, Chippewa (Ojibway) and Pottawatomie. While the latter group made its home primarily in southern Michigan, the former two made the north their home, through the Straits and Upper Peninsula. Collectively, these three tribes were known as "The Three Fires."

The stereotypical view of Native life as exemplified through countless books, stories and Hollywood "documentaries" is not applicable to the interaction among the Three Fires. They were not warlike and in fact there was little actual Native American warfare that ever occurred in Michigan. They did not wear elaborate headdresses, and did not have horses or even teepees. They were a kind and civilized people. In fact, early Jesuit missionaries noticed the natives' warm reception and love of children.

But a differing opinion is offered by the region's first newspaper, *The Manitawauba Chronicle*. Here, the paper retells the "first reliable" story about a seventeenth-century battle which allegedly occurred at the mouth of the Cheboygan River. In this account, two bands of Indians, the Ottawas and the Ausegumugs, both lived in the Straits of Mackinac region. For some "real or imagined injury," the Ausegumugs traveled south across the Straits and, while the Ottawa warriors were absent, attacked and killed two of their women. Naturally, when the Ottawa men returned, they planned to attack the Ausegumugs. Unfortunately for the Ottawa, the latter group was off warring on some other tribe, and they did not want to concentrate their efforts on slaughtering innocent women and children. Still wanting vengeance, they decided to follow the Ausegumug trail as far south as the mouth of the Cheboygan River and there hide until their homecoming.

Upon the arrival of the enemy tribe, the returning warriors began bathing themselves in the cool and refreshing waters of Lake Huron at the mouth of the river. In their opponent's ignorance the Ottawas then raised themselves up and attacked their enemy, wiping out each and every one of the Ausegumug warriors, leaving no one to carry back the heartbreaking news to the warriors' families. The *Chronicle* then assures the reader that this event "is doubtless a type of many similar events which transpired in this region...."[1] Truth be told, this story is highly improbable considering the generally peaceful nature of the Native Americans living in the area. There is little reason to believe that any such battle ever occurred in the Cheboygan area, much less that they occurred with any frequency.

At any rate, the first Europeans to arrive in the area were French explorers, fur traders and missionaries. Intrusions into North America began with explorers such as Jacques Cartier and Samuel de Champlain, who gradually made their way through the St. Lawrence Seaway in their

search for a Northwest Passage to the Orient. The first European to
visit the area, Jean Nicolet, passed through the Straits region as early as
1634 for just this purpose.[2] French fur traders then carried on the
exploration of New France and what would become Michigan, setting
up trading posts at places such as Niles, Detroit, and Michilimackinac,
the latter by about 1715. By 1669, the first mission in what would be
Michigan was set up by Père Jacques Marquette at Sault de Sainte Marie
in the Upper Peninsula.

Unfortunately for the French and Native Americans, the English
crown was beginning to take a growing interest in North America. Prime
Minister William Pitt had a particular affinity for the area and sent the
Royal Army and Navy to try and capture some of France's territorial
possessions. France, however, was greatly extended by conflicts back on
the European mainland. By 1763 and the Peace of Paris the French had
acquiesced their land claims and northern Michigan fell to the English
crown.

Native Americans were less than thrilled about the new occupiers.
They well knew the English were aspiring for territorial possession,
rather than the more benign French goals of fur and pelts. An
unsuccessful Indian revolt was led by the Ottawa chief Pontiac in 1763,
although almost all of the British forts in Michigan were captured by the
rebels, including Michilimackinac. In an ingenious plot by the Native
Americans, a group of the natives asked if they could play a game of
baggatiway (lacrosse) in honor of the king's birthday near the fort. Their
answer received in the affirmative, the game commenced. At one point
in the contest the ball "accidentally" went over the fort's wall. Indian
women, loitering near the door, furnished weapons hid under their
garments to the game's participants as they rushed in to get the ball. In
the subsequent attack, twenty-seven whites were killed and seventeen
captured.[3] In light of operations such as this, after the American war for
independence the British began a gradual retreat from Michigan.
Although they stayed as long as they possibly could, arguing that the
Americans had not fulfilled their part of the peace agreements after the
war, they could unquestionably read the writing on the wall. The British
were not welcome, and it was not worth the effort to stay.

Both the British and the Native Americans were reluctant to leave the Michigan area, but gradually both groups began to concede territorial claims. With the signing of Jay's Treaty in 1794, the British were mandated to leave by 1 June 1796; they stayed until October of that year, when American troops arrived and took the reins. In 1805 the Michigan Territory was created, and President Thomas Jefferson appointed William Hull to be its first governor.

But just as before, the Native Americans were not content with their new situation. The Americans alleged that the British in Canada were enticing rebellion at home through the Indians. In the midst of these disagreements, some such as fur trade magnate John Jacob Astor, whose American Fur Company maintained a substantial warehouse on Mackinac Island, tried to keep the peace with the natives to benefit his business.[4] Despite these efforts the frustrated American government opted for force, and so the War of 1812 began. The Americans were for the most part completely unprepared to fight, and consequently their positions were quickly compromised. Fort Mackinac, on Mackinac Island, was completely surrounded by the British; it was impossible to bring in any supplies, even water. The aggressors asked the Americans to surrender, and without firing a shot, they agreed.

In time, the British realized that it made little sense to continue this war while more significant engagements, such as a war with the French emperor Napoleon, were taking place. After a series of unfortunate losses for the British in and around the Detroit and Lake Erie region, they gave up the fight in 1814. Essentially it was now just as it was before the war, although the English were now once and for all eliminated from the Northwest Territory.

After the hostilities had ended, the United States was eager to settle its new territory. A sizeable quantity of this land was destined to be used to pay war veterans. Some two million acres in Michigan were allocated for this purpose and promptly surveyed. But not hearing encouraging reports from his surveyors, the surveyor-general of the United States, Edward Tiffin, did not hold back his opinion when describing the territory to Congress. "The whole of the two million acres appropriated in the Territory of Michigan will not contain anything like one hundred part of that quantity (that) is worth the expense of surveying it." He went on to suggest that the entire area should be abandoned.[5]

Thankfully, Congress and the President did not heed Tiffin's request. Although the United States Government owned Michigan, they still had to go through the formalities of actually acquiring the land from the Native Americans. Settlers desiring to purchase land would first visit the area, then petition the government to purchase that land. A deal would subsequently be made between government agents and Native leaders, usually involving cash, promises, trinkets, and the hope that they would not be forcibly removed later on. After these deluded proceedings had ended, the government then officially owned the land. Sadly, this had an exceedingly negative effect on Native American populations. Despite their most fervent hopes, by the 1830s the Indian population was in serious decline. A smallpox epidemic in 1837 nearly halved their numbers, and the following year forcible removal began. By 1860, only some 6,000 Native Americans remained in Michigan.[6]

The settling of Michigan by Europeans was not something which occurred with any particular rapidity. The Detroit region was already well settled, but the rest of the territory was well isolated from Michigan's only real economic center or the bustling cities of the east coast. Further problems such as lack of adequate transportation or good soil, as well as difficult living conditions further impeded settlement. These facts notwithstanding, the American phenomenon of ever wanting to move ahead and go forward would overtake these inhibitions and in time Michigan would see its fair share of settlers. The intrepid Americans became the sturdy pioneers and braved challenges incomprehensible in their quest to make a better life for themselves, their families, and their children. As a result of this settlement, in 1837 statehood was granted to Michigan under the governorship of the "Boy Governor" Stevens T. Mason. Thus the early history of the state of Michigan had come to pass, from prehistoric times until the end of the Indian presence and French and British occupation. In light of the latter, it was not long after this period that Cheboygan was settled. Indeed, the nation was still in its adolescence, and territorial expansion was yet a major objective of the United States Government. Settlement of new

areas meant the spread of American pioneerism, and with it the bold
men and women who would be responsible for taming the wilderness.

*   *   *

Three years after Michigan was admitted to the Union in 1837, the
cordoning and organization of the northernmost regions of the Lower
Peninsula began. That year, 1840, saw the organization of two counties
that would later become one of the most important lumbering regions in
the entire state. The land north of the survey line between towns thirty-
six and thirty-seven north, and east of the line between ranges four and
five west were organized into the county of Cheboygan. At the same
time, towns thirty-three through thirty-six north, range one east and one,
two and three west were laid out as the county of Wyandot, with both
attached to Mackinac County for legal and civil purposes. In 1849 the
township of Sheboygan was organized, and changed to Inverness the
following year.[7]

    In 1853 the political geography of northern Michigan began to
solidify. After a bit of redrawing, the counties of Cheboygan and
Wyandot were united into one county, Cheboygan, by an act of the state
legislature on 29 January 1853. The county seat was established at
Duncan. Taking on distinct provenance as a civil headquarters, the
counties of Presque Isle, Alpena, Montmorency, Otsego, Crawford,
Oscoda, Alcona, Iosco, Ogemaw and Roscommon were all attached to
Cheboygan for judicial purposes. Although this sounds rather dramatic,
there still was very little happening in northern Michigan. The 1860
United States Census puts Cheboygan County's population at all of 517
inhabitants.[8] Settlers were indeed coming, but not at a particularly rapid
rate, at least not yet. They needed a reason to come north, and that was
still in the works.

    Up to this point, lumbering had not yet been heavily engaged in
northern Michigan. There was little reason as yet to haul men and
equipment to a far away place when, in the early days of the state, there
were closer areas to harvest in the south. The Saginaw River Valley
became a region of particular importance for the lumber industry in
Michigan. The Muskegon River on the west side and the Tittabawassee

and Saginaw Rivers (and their tributaries) on the east side provided central Michigan with a bountiful and quality timber harvest year after year. Saginaw enjoyed a boom, and Grand Rapids became known as the furniture capital of the world. But what resulted from this, of course, was the exhaustion of available timber.[9]

The solution to this problem was to go further north. Lumbering activities sprouted up around navigable waterways to make possible the easy movement of logs to sawmills. Along the west side of the state, the northward movement of lumbering augmented growth in places such as Ludington, Manistee, Traverse City and Petoskey. Going north on the east side meant utilizing water resources such as those at the Rifle and Au Sable Rivers and Thunder Bay. Ultimately, this brought Michigan's pioneers to the Cheboygan River. This latter waterway was in an excellent position strategically. From its mouth roughly fifteen miles east of the "tip of the mitt," it would be hard to find a watercourse more ideally located to penetrate the area. But even better than that, the Cheboygan River, which empties into Lake Huron, also connects with a number of inland lakes and streams. The river itself flows directly from Mullet Lake, which then connects into Burt Lake and areas on the opposite side of the state. A few miles inland, it branches off into the Black River. It then joins to Black Lake, to which a number of other rivers and streams connect.

Would-be lumber barons saw in this extensive network of attached lakes and rivers a golden opportunity to make money from northern "green gold." Initially, however, there were some problems. The Cheboygan River, although ideally located, was too shallow for much shipping. A sand bar extending far out into the lake further complicated the problem. Nevertheless, it was still good as way to move logs out from the inland areas; once they were out of the river, they could be directed over to an ideally located bay just to the east of town, where larger ships could more easily dock and load up before making their way to Detroit, Cleveland, or Chicago. If the river were ever dredged, well, then there is no telling what might happen near its mouth. It would be an ideal location for a city.

Northern Michigan forests were well known for their excellent quality timber, especially pine, as well as the extensiveness of the woodlands. The regions were not only well-concentrated, but the wood was of especially noteworthy size. For a lumberman, a better tract of land would be difficult to find.

> The density of these northern forests is surprising. The trees grow to an immense height, and so closely together that the sun seldom penetrates their foliage. Standing in one of these clearings, and scanning the outlines of the woods, the great trunks seem so to press upon each other that one would deem it difficult for a cow to force her way into their depths.[10]

It was a superlative location for lumbering. Dense forests meant that logging operations could be concentrated in one particular area, without the hassle of long treks from camp to the day's work site. The timber itself, being of such large size, meant that more finished lumber could be had from the logs while fewer trees had to be cut down. Combine this with the aforementioned water resources, and a more nonpareil location could not be found.

Traditionally Alexander McLeod and Jacob Sammons have been given the credit as being Cheboygan's first white settlers. While this is to a certain extent true, as their arrival signified the beginnings of a community, it is not entirely accurate. Nearly lost to history is the true first settler, Captain Samuel Robertson. The skipper of a sailing vessel named the *Welcome*, Robertson was living in the late eighteenth century at Fort Mackinac on Mackinac Island. In 1778 he married fifteen-year-old Catherine "Kitty" Askin, daughter of trader John Askin and his Native American consort. Askin owned a number of vessels he used for trading with the local Indians.[11] The men had a good working relationship, with Robertson often providing assistance to Askin as he conducted his trades with the Indians near the mouth of the Cheboygan River.

An inquisitive Captain named John Shank once asked Roberson about the nature of the island and surrounding area. In a letter dated 26 April 1781, Robertson obliges the captain's request.

...to keep vessels in safety there During the Winter, the most safest place near Michilimackinac for wintering vessels is the River Shaboygan, there is six feet water upon the Barr, the River is about twenty yards wide at the entrance, & a vessel of 6 feet Draught of water cannot go up further than 200 or 300 yards, & then he can lay alongside a Clay Bank, it two fathoms of water, or she can be hove up two or three feet in mud & lay with all safety, I never saw the River freeze over or any sea to hurt a Vessel, it is clear level marshy ground for half a mile around at the mouth so that there could be no danger of them being surprised from Indians & there is always good Fishing and shooting, there is plenty of fine pines both sides of the River, & other good wood, up to the little Lake which is 3 Leagues from the mouth of it, I had a Dwelling House & Garden by the Edge of the wood and the *Welcome* wintered two winters there.[12]

Robertson offers no other information about his stay at the "River Shaboygan," but he need not say much else. The description he provides is the earliest known description of the Cheboygan River. Moreover, his letter indicates that he had settled there for two winters sometime before 1781, meaning that at the very latest he arrived in 1778 or 1779 – over sixty years before Alexander McLeod and Jacob Sammons. To Samuel Robertson must go the credit of being the area's first settler.

Another interesting aspect of this letter is that it mentions the "fine pines" of which northern Michigan would later come to be known for. The fact that he mentions that these woods extend to an inland lake is very significant. The "little Lake which is 3 Leagues from the mouth of" the river is almost assuredly what would later be known as Mullet Lake. This tells us that Robertson did his fair share of exploring while he was in the area. Whether it was for his own curiosity or part of a military assignment is not known. His geographical observations are more important than his particular reasons for doing so. In addition to the trees in the area, perfect for lumbering, Robertson also notes (indeed it is the whole reason he writes the letter) the advantageous natural harbor facilities the river provides. Up the river for a considerable distance could be secured ships of varying size, safely stored in the knowledge that they would be free from wintertime ice constriction and hull damage, not to mention Indian attacks.

While it is not known why Robertson wintered for two seasons and then left, or even exactly why he was there to begin with, his letter describing where Cheboygan would later be settled is extremely important. In just a few lines the predictive treatise describes the excellent natural harbor facilities, timberlands, waterway, fishing and hunting aspects of the area – all things which would in time become characteristically associated with the region. From a very early point the region was known for its natural advantages. It was only a matter of time before a fledgling new nation, the United States of America, expanded into this territory which was still (illegally) subject to His Britannic Majesty. The British government would eventually yield concessions to the Americans, and soon enough the locale's occupation would be discussed for the last time. By 1796 the British were gone, and northern Michigan was fully sovereign territory of the United States.[13] Activity on Mackinac Island continued for another fifty years before an entrepreneurial barrel maker drifted over from the isolated island to the mainland.

This settlement of what would become the city of Cheboygan began in the fall of 1844 when an entrepreneur named Alexander McLeod of Mackinac Island made his way across the Straits of Mackinac and landed at the mouth of the Cheboygan River. He went downstream about half a mile and built a small shanty roofed with bark. McLeod and a few of his employees wintered here as they prepared materials to use in their nascent lumber business. Not long after McLeod's arrival, a cooper from the island named Jacob Sammons sailed across the Straits. He made his way on a scow called the *Bunker Hill*, landing near the mouth of the river. Having come from Chicago that spring, he was looking for a good place to set up his business. He liked what he saw, the location being ideal for his barrel-making venture. Anticipating a more permanent relocation, Sammons built a twelve-foot square cabin a bit further up the river from McLeod's shanty. In the spring Sammons returned to get his family and employees, and thus they became Cheboygan's first permanent residents.[14]

Meanwhile, shortly after his arrival, McLeod built a dam and soon had in operation a small water-powered saw. He had brought with him a number of men to help him in his new endeavor, and by the fall of 1846 this small enterprise had shipped the first lumber out of what would be Cheboygan. They sent some 500,000 feet of lumber to Chicago, indeed not bad for a start (although later a number of mills would be able to cut that much each in five days!)[15] With the huge amount of timber in the north, there would certainly be no shortage of materials with which to apply his trade. The supply of quality wood was, at this time, essentially unlimited. Lumber – and plenty of it – was sparking a manufacturing and social revolution in northern Michigan. Business had begun in Cheboygan.

The name itself, "Cheboygan," is of unknown, or rather greatly hypothesized, origin. It appears as early as 1792 on a British map of the area which depicts the "Sheboigan River."[16] As previously discussed, the area was native to the Chippewa Indians, also known as "Cehboys". "Gan" is the Chippewa term for water, and so the name may mean Chippewa Water.[17] Another conjecture is that it comes from an abbreviation of "kitchi" (great), and "poygan" (pipe). There is yet another possibility, and that is a derivation of the French spelling of the river's name, Kichibwagan. An additional explanation is a derivation of Zee-bwa-gan, meaning cane or hollow bone. A more popular legend, however, and perhaps the most often told, is one that involves a bit of folklore. It is the one probably least likely, but the most entertaining.[18] An old Indian chief, having already fathered several sons but no daughter, was eagerly awaiting the arrival of his first baby girl. But when his wife gave birth it was yet again a boy, and he walked away in disgust, saying, "She's a boy again." This colorful story actually originated much later on the docks at Mackinac Island. An Indian, dressed as a chief, greeted tourists with bits of local folklore, this being but one of them. A representation of this is illustrated on the cover of the 1898 booklet *Cheboygan, Up-to-Date*.[19] Other explanations of the origin of the name exist. Whatever the case may be the name "Cheboygan" eventually stuck and became one with the expanding settlement.

Subsequent settlers quickly followed after the initial pioneers of McLeod and Sammons. Stemming from the new lumber mill, other businesses soon began to pop up. The availability of lumber brought men such as Stebbens Winchell and shipbuilder John Vincent and their families to the area, who settled on the east and west sides of the river, respectively. Vincent soon built the first ship ever constructed in Cheboygan, with the construction of the sloop-rigged scow *Elizabeth* in 1847.[20] As early as 1845 a blacksmith shop had been set up in Cheboygan. The proprietors, named Ring and Marble, were only in operation for a brief stint. Ring (and possibly Marble as well) was involved in a counterfeiting scheme involving the manufacturing of dubious ten cent pieces and half dollars. Not surprisingly, they quickly quit town and "left for parts unknown." A more reputable blacksmith, Peter LaBelle, came to the community in 1848, working for Alexander McLeod.[21]

In September 1848, Sammons became the owner of what later would become downtown Cheboygan when the United States General Land Office in Genesee issued him three land patents. This land was platted in 1851 and contained forty-five lots and was named "Cheboygan."[22] With these patents now in hand, Jacob Sammons became the owner of a significant section of a town that would soon become one of the greatest lumbering communities in the north.

Although not even four years had passed since Sammons first set himself up on the river, the first arrest was made in early 1848. "One James Jacket, in the employ of Sammons and Granger, was the victim. James had a set-to with one Buchanan, for which he was arrested and taken to Mackinac and fined before a justice of the peace. J. B. Spencer being the constable who made the arrest."[23] This seemingly insignificant squabble was not so trivial. The need for justice signified the more direct interactions people were having with each other, and consequently was reflective of the augmentation of the northern settlement. The same year also saw the establishment of the first schoolhouse, which was built on the corner of what today is Main and Pine streets. There were twelve pupils that inaugural year, with Miss Harriet McLeod in charge of educating the students.[24] Subsequent school buildings (parochial and public) popped up as they were needed, steadily increasing in number with the growing number of settlers and their children.

Meanwhile, the operations of the area were becoming increasingly noteworthy, both in terms of lumber cut and men employed. The A. & R. McLeod enterprise employed thirty men and their mill was valued at $14,000 in 1850. It contained two upright saws, producing 1,500,000 board feet of lumber annually. (A board foot is a one foot square piece of wood, one inch thick). In 1847 the area's second mill was built. Combined, these two mills produced 13,000,000 feet of lumber during the period in which they were in operation. As one historian has expressed, "Clearly these were the precursors of the 'monster' mills of the next decade."[25] Over the next few years, the community began to grow. Soon more small sawmills, cooper and blacksmith shops, hotels and other businesses gradually opened up in the newly settled area. On 16 December 1850 a post office was established at nearby Duncan City, with Alexander McLeod taking the reins as the first postmaster.[26] Passenger ships also began to service the Cheboygan area, although it would still be some time before the railroads made their way north. This growth, while very significant, would pale in comparison to the growth that would take place in just a few years. Indeed, Cheboygan was well on its way to becoming much more prosperous. The lumber was available and the workers were coming to settle in this new community. And with the lumbermen would come their families and, consequently, the need for grocers, blacksmiths, novelty stores, tobacconists, and all those who would be a necessary part of day-to-day existence.

Another aspect of daily life that accompanied the new settlers was their religion. From Cheboygan's very early days, religion quickly gained a foothold in the community which continues to this day. Throughout the various changes that have taken place in the community, her churches have been there to care for the spiritual needs of her citizens. The first religious service in Cheboygan was held in 1852 at the house of Charles Bellant by Fr. Andrew D.J. Piret, a Belgian by birth but living at the time on Mackinac Island. At this point there were still a limited number of families in Cheboygan, as well as a few single men employed in the mill, who all were thankful for Fr. Piret's services.[27] In the interim before the first permanent facilities were established, missionaries carried out most of the religious duties. One in particular, Fr. Angelles Van Pamel, baptized several children in the presence of a bishop from

THE UNITED STATES OF AMERICA,

To all to whom these Presents shall come, Greeting:

CERTIFICATE No. 2210

WHEREAS *Jacob Sammons of Mackinaw County, Michigan,*

has deposited in the GENERAL LAND OFFICE of the United States, a Certificate of the REGISTER OF THE LAND OFFICE at *Genesee* whereby it appears that full payment has been made by the said *Jacob Sammons,*

according to the provisions of the Act of Congress of the 24th of April, 1820, entitled "An Act making further provision for the sale of the Public Lands," for *the South West part of the South West fractional quarter of Section twenty nine, in Township thirty eight, North, of Range One, West, in the District of Lands subject to sale at Genesee, Michigan, containing fourteen acres, and eighty five hundredths of an acre,*

according to the official plat of the survey of the said Lands, returned to the General Land Office by the SURVEYOR GENERAL, which said tract has been purchased by the said *Jacob Sammons,*

NOW KNOW YE, That the United States of America, in consideration of the Premises, and in conformity with the several acts of Congress, in such case made and provided, HAVE GIVEN AND GRANTED, and by these presents DO GIVE AND GRANT, unto the said *Jacob Sammons,*

and to his heirs, the said tract above described: TO HAVE AND TO HOLD the same, together with all the rights, privileges, immunities, and appurtenances of whatsoever nature, thereunto belonging, unto the said *Jacob Sammons,* and to his heirs and assigns forever.

In Testimony Whereof, I, *James K. Polk* PRESIDENT OF THE UNITED STATES OF AMERICA, have caused these Letters to be made PATENT, and the SEAL of the GENERAL LAND OFFICE to be hereunto affixed.

GIVEN under my hand, at the CITY OF WASHINGTON, the *first* day of *September* in the year of our Lord one thousand eight hundred and *forty eight* and of the INDEPENDENCE OF THE UNITED STATES the *Seventy third.*

BY THE PRESIDENT: *James K. Polk*

By *J. K. Mathews* Sec'y.

S. H. Laughlin RECORDER of the General Land Office.

Image of Jacob Sammon's first land patent to what would later become downtown Cheboygan, dated 1 September 1848 (Image courtesy United States Bureau of Land Management).

Detroit and an Indian chief with some twenty other Indians.[28]

Missionaries alone would not be enough to handle Cheboygan's growing population, still mostly Catholic at this point. By 1856 the first chapel was built, under the direction of the zealous missionary Fredrick Baraga.[29] Later, in 1869, construction of the current church began, on property which was donated by Sanford Baker.[30] It was completed "as the means of the congregation would permit," which finally took place in 1875.[31] Religious services continued in the area with greater frequency as the population steadily increased.

Meanwhile, to the east of town lay the village of Duncan City (sometimes referred to simply as Duncan). Its founder, Jeremiah Woolston Duncan, had previously realized how valuable the northern timberlands could be. Born in Baltimore, Maryland in 1810, he was an intrepid and prodigious entrepreneur from a young age. "While still but a boy in years"[32] he went to Philadelphia and found employment as a clerk. He became a businessman at age twenty when he entered into a partnership with his brother John selling hardware. He was not involved in this venture for long, though, and by 1830 he was directing his attention to lumbering. In 1849 he bought into McLeod's holdings when he purchased the mill and surrounding property at Duncan Bay, or McLeod's Bay as it was known at the time. The following year he moved to Chicago and devoted all his efforts to lumbering. He purchased large tracts of land (including that at Duncan Bay), being almost entirely financed by two gentlemen named Alfred and Jeremiah Woolston.[33] Duncan was typical of northern Michigan lumbermen in the respect that he was financed by means other than himself. Rarely did a lumberman make his fortune by paying for everything out of his own pocket. Often too big of an expense for one man, financing usually came from already wealthy lumber barons or optimistic businessmen in major cities along the eastern seaboard or in Chicago.

Duncan, together with McLeod (who soon sold a controlling interest in the operations to Duncan in 1849 or 1850), were both eager to become prosperous lumber barons themselves, and so got to work right away. Duncan made technological improvements to the existing mill when he installed new Muley saws and added a siding mill to the facility.[34] They now had the ability to go through a greater amount of lumber and to process it more efficiently.

Unfortunately, not all their lumbering operations were exactly legal. In 1849 the United States government seized a sizable quantity of logs Duncan and McLeod had cut. This was of course their own fault, considering the timber had been cut from federal land.[35] Such seizures were not at all uncommon among early lumbering operations. Sometimes timber was cut accidentally off government-owned lands, and sometimes more unscrupulously harvested. While in the woods cutting and hauling logs, it was very easy to lose track of where exactly one was located, so drifting over a property line, even a considerable distance over, was not difficult. This run-in with Uncle Sam was perhaps not the greatest way to start a business, but the setback was very short-lived.

Duncan was not one to be easily deterred. In light of this, he purchased a sizeable piece of land on the west shore of what would later be Duncan Bay in February of 1852. The next year the construction of a new, larger mill began.[36] Duncan's community of workers and their families living near the mill soon became known as Duncan City, near the end of what today is Duncan Avenue. Interestingly, many of the settlers here were of Swedish decent. Duncan, looking for workers for his new 'city,' was able to secure through immigration authorities a boatload of new arrivals from the Scandinavian nation. Among the many different ethnic groups which eventually settled in the region, the Swedish were the first to settle here in large numbers.[37] Clearly Duncan intended to make this a very permanent settlement.

Cheboygan and Duncan City were ideally close to one another, but traveling between the two could be a significant hassle. To remedy this, the communities were united in 1852 when Duncan built a direct road between Duncan City and the watermill at the Cheboygan rapids (present-day Duncan Avenue). This made it possible for people to either live or work at either place, while always remaining close to the action in the cities. In the years following this mini-boom, lumber production increased and both Cheboygan and Duncan reaped the rewards. Duncan City, completely on the water and more accessible by ship, became the more significant settlement of the two, though both enjoyed accelerated

Jeremiah Woolston Duncan (Image courtesy Ellis Olson / Scharf, *History of Delaware*).

growth. In 1853 Duncan City became the county seat, where it remained until 1856, when it was moved to Cheboygan.[38]

By the beginning of the 1850s it was clear that northern Michigan was well on its way to becoming an important place for harvesting the state's timber resources. All the conditions – geographically and economically – were right for Cheboygan's growth. By now enough people had settled to establish a crucially important economic base. From here the place could grow.

A number of events soon transpired which indicated the growth the tip of the mitt settlements were enjoying. In 1850 Cheboygan's Main Street was laid out and the following year the first steamboat, the *Stockman*, touched at the village. A boat soon made its first appearance farther up the river as well, with the arrival of the *Columbia*.[39] Shipping, the only really viable means of transportation at this time, was increasing in frequency at the new settlement. With these ships would also come increased commerce, both in terms of industry and seasonal guests.

The only way ships would continue to dock was if they had some safe means to do so. In light of this, in 1851 the first lighthouse was built in the area. This beacon, the Cheboygan Main Light, was constructed at the east end of Duncan Bay by two gentlemen named Rhodes and Warner of Ohio. It had a white tower with spiral staircase, about forty feet high and separate from the keeper's quarters, at the top of which was as a revolving fifth-order Fresnel lens made by L. Saultier and Company of Paris, France. William Drew was the first keeper of the light. This beacon "…at once emphasized the importance of the locality as one of the most secure harbors of refuge for lake marine," not to mention how important it would be for commercial shipping.[40] Unfortunately, by 1859 the low ground on which the tower had been built was being flooded so much that the stone foundation of the light became unsafe, and the tower had to be removed. The new light, built on the same location, was an eight-foot square wooden tower resting on top of a two story, eight room dwelling. The light's new height was thirty-three feet and employed the same light that was in the previous tower.[41] The erection of this light, so soon after the arrival of Cheboygan and Duncan City's first settlers, shows the speed with which the area was becoming increasingly important. To would-be lumber barons and settlers of all types, the region was attracting plenty of attention, which would be essential for further growth.

Sadly, this development was soon dealt a noteworthy setback. The unexpected death of Jeremiah Duncan in 1854 dealt a severe blow to the area. As the proprietor of the only mill of real substance at this time, his death meant that there was no one left to operate it. He had left one of his brothers as executor of the estate, but in 1856 he forcibly suspended his late brother's business operations. What happened next is not nearly as clear, but it appears that the mills and property reverted back to the state for non-payment of taxes. While work on the mill continued and was completed in 1855, many of the men who built it were not paid for their work.[42] After all, no one was really sure what was going to happen to the mill. Men who were depending on the hard-earned fruits of their labor were left without compensation. In the still rather remote north, this would have been exceedingly detrimental, considering the great lengths that many of Duncan's employees had taken to come to northern Michigan. His death, while not a permanent hindrance, did for a time cause a severe disruption to further expansion of the area.

Although the premature death of Jeremiah Duncan was most inopportune, many of the early settlers had their livelihoods as a result of his pioneering spirit. While there would be stagnation in the area for several years, Duncan had already done a great deal to help the area. Although still in its infancy, the combined Cheboygan and Duncan City site had been well established as a lumbering community. Only more time and people stood in the way of progress now, and it would not be long before sufficient quantities of both were in place to see to it that the north grew.

2

The Growth of the Community

The initial pioneers of the area did not have an easy future ahead of them. While Cheboygan and Duncan City had been well established, a few things were holding the communities back. Transportation facilities to the north were still limited, as were the number of workers, and the death of Jeremiah Duncan had left a major business' fate to be decided in the courts. Consequently, for the next ten years, there was very little growth in Cheboygan (by 1870 the population was still only 800).[1] The complications after Jeremiah Duncan's death which caused his company to close its doors consequently caused great complications for the greater economy of the area. Fortunately this stagnation did not last forever. The state sold the land around the mills to other outside businessmen and they soon opened back up. Even a United States Land Office would be soon be located in Duncan City, not to mention the fact that it was the seat of government of still tiny Cheboygan County. The progress continued in 1866 when the village was made a port of entry.[2]

But before Duncan City and the area as a whole could regain its status as an important community once again, the stagnation which Duncan's death had caused had to be remedied. An Englishman named Sanford Baker was just the answer the area needed. The details are sketchy about just how major a role Baker played in the development of Duncan City, due to the brief time he was a part of its history. What is known is that Baker arrived in Michigan in 1867 from Oneida County, New York, where he had settled on a homestead. Upon making the trek west, Baker was able to then purchase much of the disputed land from the Duncan estate which had since fallen back into the hands of the state. He purchased this property in collaboration with Archibald Thompson and Robert Patterson. The three men then breathed new life into Duncan City, whose buildings had become since Duncan's death "little more than wrecks."[3] Baker's son, Harry, told of his father's arrival in the north:

> When he arrived there was nothing at Duncan but an old idle mill that had fallen into disrepair. My father developed a splendid town there. He built two sawmills and docks, besides camps, and a boarding house. A company store was established. Mill workers built homes, and the government opened a post office...[4]

Presumably, the post office that had originally been established in 1850 closed shortly after Duncan died. Once Baker arrived on the scene, the area began thriving once again, with no small amount of credit due to this immigrant from New York.

The very next year, Thompson and Patterson sold their interests to Mears & Company of Chicago, and the name was changed to Baker, Mears & Company. In 1870 Thompson Smith purchased the Mears & Company land around Duncan Bay. It is after this sale that the real boom of Duncan City began. Smith, a true father of the community, was an able and generous businessman. He was "persevering, not easily discouraged, confident in adversity and cheerful under losses that would have dismayed others," all characteristics which would help him a great deal in northern Michigan. The son of a Revolutionary War veteran, Smith began his career lumbering in Canada and operating a mill in Albany, New York. He then came to Duncan City and rebuilt or constructed many new buildings at the site, all for his lumbering operations. He built a foundry, machine, wagon and blacksmith shops, and many other facilities. He also owned many houses which his workers rented. Essentially Duncan City was a one-man, company town, and Thompson Smith was both lord and moral authority. He allowed no alcohol in his town, and considering he owned virtually all the buildings there, it was a relatively easy law to dictate.[5] How well it was obeyed, however, is another story altogether. Booze was freely available in Cheboygan, just a quick ride away.

Despite all this development which occurred quite rapidly, Baker did not stick around long. Shortly after the mini-boom of which he was part, he sold half of his share to lumbermen Smith and a returning Robert Patterson. By 1877, Smith, Baker, and Patterson dissolved their partnership and took land in exchange for their interests in the mills. Thompson Smith and his sons, Ephraim and Egbert, kept the Duncan City property and some 10,000 acres and continued to build up the settlement around the mills.[6] Later, after fire destroyed one of the original mills, a new one was built which became one of the largest of its type in the entire state. Baker, meanwhile, took as his share of the property land which was located on the west side of the Cheboygan River, located within the village.[7]

Down the street in Cheboygan, things were gradually getting better there as well. In 1863 a small bridge was constructed at Third Street (what is today State Street), linking the east and west sides of the river nearer the mouth. It was completed at a cost of $766.15. A few years later, in 1869, a regular steamboat connection was established with the arrival of the side-wheeled steamer *Marine City*. This steamboat sailed between Cleveland, Detroit and Mackinac Island and called in Cheboygan each way.[8] This was a particularly significant event, as it meant that Cheboygan now had regular contact with not only the hustle and bustle of Detroit and Cleveland (important shipping cities in their own right), but also because now tourists and businessmen could make frequent, planned trips to northern Michigan. Moreover, northern residents also now had greater flexibility and freedom, being able to travel with ease, should their means or needs permit. Things were once again looking up for Cheboygan, Duncan City, and the surrounding region.

Although it was a feat in and of itself to get ships to land at Cheboygan and Duncan City, up until this point there were but few transportation options for one who wanted to come north. Because of its remoteness, the only realistic way to get there was by boat. In 1861, however, the State of Michigan enacted a law providing for the construction of twenty-three state roads. Specifically, it called for the building of "A road from Duncan, in Cheboygan county [sic], to Sauble river, in Iosco county, via Alpena, to be known as the Duncan, Alpena and Sauble river State road."[9] Further progress was made in 1869 when the road was ordered extended from Cheboygan to the Old Mackinaw and Little Traverse Bay State Road. Two years later an additional State Road was laid out as the Cheboygan and Little Traverse Bay State Road.[10] The construction of these roads, while definitely important for any would-be settler in northern Michigan, did come with one significant caveat. They were often little more than dirt tracks which occasionally provided the traveler with the luxury of a corrugated surface via buried logs. Given this option it is no surprise .that steamboats were still the preferred method of travel until the arrival of the railroad in 1881. Nevertheless, a number of stagecoach lines provided services on these roads, including those of Ivory Littlefield, Allison, and Charles Carrow.[11] Transport on these roads was relatively limited unless there was a very good reason to come north and sailing was not an option.

Sanford Baker's share of the Duncan estate was not the only one to fall into entrepreneurial lumbermen's hands. One of the most pivotal players in Cheboygan's history, which got its start from the Duncan estate, was the firm of W. & A. McArthur Company, Limited. Yet another group of investors from New York including George W. Swan, John R. McArthur, Lucius Southwick and John F. McDonald purchased, in 1865, a portion of the late Jeremiah Duncan's estate. Vast tracts of land were purchased for negligible amounts when compared to the amount that they were actually worth in terms of marketable timber standing on the land. This property included some 14,000 acres of pine timber, various buildings, and mills in Duncan City and Cheboygan. The newly formed organization was known as McArthur, Southwick and Co. Promptly, the company began the production of lumber and shingles, while repairing the mill and dam at the Cheboygan River site. This was an extremely pivotal moment in the nascent history of Cheboygan. As it is described in the late nineteenth century work *The Traverse Region, Historical and Descriptive, Illustrated*, "It will be observed that as the organization of this industry became perfected, the various elements of a

The W. & A. McArthur Mill, about 1885 (Image courtesy Ellis Olson).

business center combined, and by 1869 the village [of Cheboygan] began to take shape and grew rapidly."[12]

In July of 1866 William McArthur, son of John R. McArthur, purchased Southwick's share of the company. The same year they built a shingle mill at the Cheboygan site, which later was converted to a grist mill. In 1867, Ward B. McArthur, a nephew of John R. McArthur, purchased part of John F. McDonald's interest. By 1869 the company had completed a canal eighteen feet wide by eighty feet long, and with a lift of nine feet. By the close of the decade, the McArthur Company had also constructed a large water mill and around the same time divided or sold twelve hundred acres around Duncan City and the village proper.[13] In sum, within just four years they had etched out a big portion of the local lumber market for themselves and played an important role in everyone else's use of the river.

In 1867, this same group had organized the Cheboygan Slack Water Navigation Company. This boom company was extremely important in that it allowed proper utilization of the river for everyone. The purpose of a boom company was, as authorized by law, "for the purposes of engaging in and carrying on the business of running, driving, booming and rafting logs, timber, lumber and other floatables..."[14] A boom company sorted out floating timber as it made its way from lumber camps further along the river. These camps along the river naturally belonged to any number of companies, and when the spring thaws came the neatly stacked logs from the winter cutting season were released to float down to the mills. The result could be chaotic, with dozens of companies' logs in the river at any one time. The boom company made sense of the floating mass by identifying each log to its owner through the use of logmarks. These unique brands, usually applied with a device that looked like a cross between a pickaxe and a hammer, carried on the end a registered mark which would be struck into a company's log. When they got to the boom, they could easily be sorted according to the owner by looking at the mark thereon. Individual booms or bays were set up for each company so that all their logs could be grouped together. Once a significant amount had been collected, they were bound together with heavy chains or hemp rope and rafted en masse down to the owner's mill (using a tugboat if necessary), providing they had paid the necessary booming fees.[15] Otherwise, the boom company got the logs.

But before much else happened in Cheboygan, something was going to have to be done about the river. Although a fine waterway in terms of width, the mouth was only four feet deep, hardly enough for swimming, let alone for shipping millions of feet of lumber. Duncan City had provided a much more ideal shipping location, and that is why up to this point the more important place had been there and not Cheboygan. The obvious advantage of the river, however, was bound to be utilized. In 1874 the United States Congress allocated funds for the dredging of the river. The operation, led by U.S. engineer Roy Cram, was to dredge 32,000 cubic yards at the mouth of the river at twenty-eight cents per yard. Six years later, a second operation deepened the river to eighteen feet from the mouth of the river to what is today the State Street Bridge. The deep section from the Straits to the bridge now measured about a mile and a half. Another project in 1907 dredged the river from the bridge to the locks. In sum, 11,720 feet of channel was improved (6,000 in the Straits), making the Cheboygan river much more navigable and, consequently, making the place a much more attractive locale to build any number of mills or factories.[16] Shipping was no longer a problem since the river had been dredged, and the ease of access to it forever changed the subsequent history of the community.

At about the same time as these events were transpiring, a William Smith of Westfield, New York, purchased John R. McArthur and George W. Swan's interest in the McArthur Company. Changing names yet again, it became known as McArthur, Smith & Co. Improvements continued to the facilities, and in 1876 a dock and warehouse business was started near the mouth of the river's west side. The company also then began dealing in coal, salt, and lime, in addition to lumber. They provided "as good dockage facilities as are found on the lakes." Of great benefit to the company was the fact that they also owned a lumber yard in Chicago, under the direction of Archibald McArthur.[17]

McArthur, Smith & Co., despite being the most important mill operators in Cheboygan at this time, also caused their fair share of problems. Before the adoption of the band saw in the 1880s, circular saws like those in use all over the state were incredibly wasteful. They generated enormous quantities of sawdust as refuse.[18] Daily operations produced large amounts of the unwanted and unneeded byproduct which had to be disposed of. What was McArthur, Smith & Co.'s solution to the problem? Dump it in the river. They maintained that the waste was through "the swiftness and strength of the river's current carried harmlessly far out into the Lake [sic]...." Other Cheboyganites, both man and beast, tended to have different opinions.

> On the other hand, our beautiful river, taking its source as it does from numerous springs of deliciously pure water, is the Croton water-works for all Cheboygan; for laundry purposes it is almost equal to rain water, and for culinary uses very palatable, but for the mealy thickness of genuine pulverized saw-logs. The fish, too, that were found in goodly numbers ready, - almost waiting to be caught, have taken such offence at the flavor of saw-dust extract, in their natural beverage, that they have fled away in disgust; in fact were a profound Geologist to examine the bed of our river he would have first to bore through a strata of saw-dust, the thickness of at least one or two A. No. 1 saw-logs, for the sacred soil of this flying river which will not carry this offending powder where it ought to go – out of everybody's way.[19]

In addition to the sawdust polluting the fishes' natural beverage, it also created more significant problems. One Cheboygan ship, the *Grace Dormer*, had the feed pipes for her boilers so plugged with drawn in waste that she could not draw enough water to make steam to operate.[20] This counterproductive means of waste disposal was eventually prohibited, as there was no way it could reasonably continue. Once it was eventually outlawed, the McArthur, Smith & Co. had to find another way to get rid of their rubbish.

The problems that came with dealing such large quantities of sawdust should not be underestimated. The McArthur Company's eventual solution to the problem, disposing of it in a large pile on the opposite side of the river, was perhaps a rudimentary solution at best. Although it was fast, the circular saws in use at this time also became increasingly wasteful the more they were used. Saws of five-sixteenth inch bite would turn 312 feet of wood per thousand into sawdust, or nearly a half-inch of log per board. Once band saws were developed, however, this number was reduced to eighty-three feet per thousand.[21] Innovations such as this were of great benefit not only to the McArthur Company, but to all lumber barons and mill operators both large and small. Less waste meant more wood went to market, not to mention the fact that they now had less garbage on had to try and dispose of.

The company, meanwhile, continued with its business. Ward B. McArthur died in 1879, and three years later, in 1882, William and Archibald McArthur purchased all shares and interests in the business, renaming it (for the last time) the W. & A. McArthur Company, Limited. Under William's control, "The buildings and property of the firm not only bespeak excellent business management but are of a character that reflect credit upon the community."[22] The firm grew quickly with William at the helm, and developed into a place of prominence and importance as Cheboygan matured.

The McArthurs are not at all unlike other lumbermen who came to Michigan. Both William and Archibald spent much of their younger days at Mt. Morris, New York, where the McArthur sons first learned how to be effective businessmen. The two brothers had been carrying on the family business, being partners in a public works contracting started by their father, the aforementioned John R. McArthur. John apparently had a passing interest in lumber which rubbed off on his sons, and they gradually became interested enough to delve into that industry themselves. Ward bought into the public works business about a year after William and (presumably) Archibald did in 1866.[23] Many of the lumber barons who lived and conducted their operations in Cheboygan and Michigan in general came from the eastern states. New England had had an excellent pine belt, from which many men had made fortunes. But when this gave out, they had to move west. Michigan was right in this belt, and so became a natural haven for those who would do their best to make money from the woods. This was the opportunity that the McArthur boys, and others, jumped on.

Meanwhile, things continued to boom in Duncan City as well. In 1870, Thompson Smith bought the mills, buildings, and land from McArthur, Southwick and Company at Duncan City which had formerly been owned by the late Jeremiah W. Duncan. Smith soon began his operations there.[24] His largest facility, greatly expanded from Duncan's, aptly earned the title of "Big Mill." And indeed it was – this new mill was one of the largest in the state (at 45,000 square feet), and valued at the time at $150,000.[25] Its processing capacity was an astounding 350,000 feet of lumber every ten hours.[26] The presence of such a large mill in addition to an already established one is indicative not only of the amount of lumber that was present in the area (and indeed all of northern Michigan), but also of the belief that this would be a viable area to be in for a good many years to come, as far as lumbering was concerned. With that in mind, Smith also understood the necessity of treating his workers reasonably well. According to the late Gordon Turner, Smith "allowed workers to take short ends of lumber from his mill and construct homes for themselves, and to take log trimming for fuel. He charged rent of $2 to $3 a month."[27] Nevertheless, the work at Smith's mill (as in any mill) was difficult by every sense of the word.

As if the Big Mill was not enough, adjoining it was another facility called the "Little Mill." This mill was not used as extensively as the Big Mill was. Not only was it physically older, but it also contained older equipment, such as circular saws, which had since been outdated by more efficient band saws. It did, however, sport one edger, trimmer, and a lathe mill. A twelve foot high platform and tramway surrounded both mills and extended far onto four of the five docks which jetted out into the bay (the other was for steamboat dockings and freight storage).[28] Between the two mills, docks, and stacked lumber, virtually the entire Duncan City waterfront was covered by some aspect of the Thompson Smith lumber mills. But perhaps more importantly, no facet of Duncan City was detached from them, either. Everything in town existed for the mills and their operations exclusively. Mills, stables, storehouses, the general store – everything was directly related to the Thompson Smith Company.

One particular job which was arguably more important than any other, even the workers in the mill, was the one which could help assure that Duncan City's inhabitants would continue to be able to sustain their livelihoods. Firefighters – those who could defend house and mill alike – had a place of pivotal importance in Duncan City. All fire protection equipment was all located close to the mills, but yet was in a central enough location that firefighters could get to anywhere in town if their services were needed. The city fire department consisted of eighteen men plus one chief. The men were drilled weekly, and had nine carts with hoses of 3600 feet total length at their disposal. Within the mill facilities, additional fire equipment was well-placed at potentially problematic locations. There were also operating within the mill four nightly watchmen with ten different checkpoints, and a comprehensive assortment of various firefighting apparatus. As if that was not enough, Smith provided other equipment as well. One of his tugs, the *Duncan City* (a sizeable vessel at 179 gross tons), could project four two and a half inch streams of water onto an incendiary crisis. An additional tug could throw three more streams onto any impending disaster.[29]

Thompson Smith's operations are remarkable even for their time. When other mills were typically processing around 100,000 feet of timber per day, Smith and his sons as successors were producing well over three times that amount. (The company was renamed Thompson Smith's Sons after their father's death in December 1884). It also cannot be ignored that despite any early reason for Duncan City's settlement, the present reality was that the city existed almost entirely for the support of his mills. Needing lots of timber, he often got it from a

considerable distance away, including the Rogers City area, some forty
miles to the east of where his mill was located. In total, the vast holdings
of the company totaled around 14,000 acres.[30] This tells us not only that
it was necessary to go to great lengths to get lumber, but probably more
significantly that the Thompson Smith Company was so large that the
community of Duncan City simply could not survive without it. In and
of itself this was a dangerous situation – if there was ever a fire in
Duncan City which destroyed the mills, the settlement as a whole would
be doomed.

The lifestyle for most of those earning a living in any one of the
local mills and the area in general would have been hardly the ideal.
Working in the mills was hard and demanding, and with little
communication with the rest of the world, one could feel isolated in
these remote northern communities. Local historian Ellis Olson paints
the picture:

> It is difficult, today, to visualize Cheboygan during its first few
> years of growth. Its scattered homes lying alongside the few
> dirt roads, lacking even the crudest type of sidewalk, would
> hardly be the picture of prosperity. Good paint was still a thing
> of the future so buildings were either left bare or were
> whitewashed…. Odors of burning pitch mushroomed from
> the chimneys of the quaint dwellings. Women doing their
> weekly wash on the riverbank and the men piling lumber on
> the docks were common scenes during those early days.[31]

Life was simple but still tough. There was always plenty of work to be
done. This was complicated by the fact that Cheboygan and Duncan
City were still both relatively small and outside the realm of the rest of
the state of Michigan, with most of the activity further south in Detroit
and the Saginaw Valley. Nevertheless, rapid growth continued in the
north – between the years 1870 and 1871, Cheboygan's population grew
over 180%.[32]

The growing numbers of settlers in Cheboygan were coming here
first and foremost to work. But what they were doing, of course, was
much more than that. They were also forming a tightly-knit community,

an association of settlers of which all local people were a member. While clearly founded to cut wood, the city was becoming a more vibrant, cultured place. In 1877 the people of Cheboygan erected the celebrated Opera House / City Hall building. The nexus of social interface in the community, the Opera House immediately became a popular place for varied forms of entertainment. Located on the same site today, the facility remains an excellent compliment to a refined downtown, what once was merely a scattered spattering of small homes and mills. The Opera House was built at the corner of Huron and Backus Streets in the downtown area, just off of Main Street. In the rear of the building was the City Hall and county jail, conducting the daily legal affairs of the community. It was a most welcome addition to the now much more refined village.

The seemingly exponential growth of the populace also predicated the establishment of more religious organizations. In October 1868 the First Methodist Episcopal Church was established in Cheboygan, with the church being dedicated in August 1872. Rev. William Riley was its first pastor. The Congregationalist Church was then organized in December, 1871, and the St. James Episcopal Church followed in 1879. By the middle of the 1880s, Baptists, Lutherans and independent Christians were all represented in the community.[33]

The late 1860s and early 1870s saw great evolution in Cheboygan's continued growth, although in some ways the area was still lacking. Up until this point there were still but few transportation options for one who wanted to come north. In 1868 work began on a lock on the Cheboygan River and was completed in the following year.[34] With both the river dredged and new locks in place, the sprouting community was lacking in nothing. Men, capital, and resources were all already present or were within just a few years of arriving in town. There was absolutely nothing to hold the city back as the lumber boom continued and the rest of the state and nation called for the raw materials it could produce with amazing quality, speed and efficiency.

Thus, as the 1870s began, things were progressing rapidly for Cheboygan. In February of 1870, the post office at Duncan City was officially changed to Cheboygan, with Francis M. Sammons as the new postmaster.[35] On 9 May 1871, the village of Cheboygan was officially organized, with W.P. Maiden, M.D., as president.[36] Meanwhile, by the next year annual lumber production, in board feet, had reached 35,000,000, as compared to 500,000 in 1846 (McArthur, Smith & Co. alone provided 15,000,000 board feet in annual production).[37] By 1876, fifteen kerosene-burning lamps were illuminating the community, and the following year the area was officially reincorporated as a village (due to a technicality in state law).[38] At this time there were around fifty mills, six hotels, as well as other foundries, stores, and shops. There were two newspapers, three lawyers, and a Western Union telegraph station.[39] But what is perhaps more important is that this decade provided the foundation upon which the real boom period of the next two decades would be built on. Indeed it was this time that would make future success possible.

> Over 25 sawmills were constructed, enlarged, or replaced in Cheboygan during the 1870s. Although this was not the period which produced the most lumber, it was a time of great building and of preparation for things to come. Undoubtedly, the dredging of the river, the construction of the locks, and the incorporation of the Village had the profoundest effect on the lumbering business.[40]

The 1870s was a period in Cheboygan in which things had finally started to materialize. The village had broken free of its stagnation caused by the death of Jeremiah Duncan, the shallowness of the river, and the lack of lumber mills to draw large numbers of working men and their families. The period of the most lumber production was still over a decade off, but the growth in Cheboygan during the 1870s served as the catalyst which was necessary for its further augmentation.

What is needed in any community is a reason for would-be inhabitants to move there in the first place. Usually, this comes from an availability of jobs. Now that there were lumber mills in Cheboygan, and fine facilities for shipping that lumber, there was no shortage of employment opportunities. As the workers came, they brought their families, and soon other businesses began popping up as well. Elevating the town beyond frontier status, these new settlers came and built more than just mills and saloons. They built hotels, banks, and professional buildings. They brought in more transportation facilities, and made physical improvements to the downtown. Lumber made all of this possible, but now the community was beginning to take on a sense of greater permanence. As the 1870s faded to the prospects of the 1880s, the village of Cheboygan increased in both size and significance.

3

The Boom Begins

By the 1880s, the northern settlements at Duncan City and Cheboygan were making excellent headway in their strive towards becoming more stable and lasting communities. More and more lumbering interests were making their way north to commence operations in the virgin timberlands of Cheboygan County. Because of what Cheboygan and Duncan City were consequently becoming, and as a natural result of frontier expansion, it became necessary to increase transportation options to and from the area. While shipping may be enough for a limited quantity of lumber, the perpetually increasing board footage per year mandated that an alternate form of transportation be devised. What is more, the area was also becoming a popular area with resorters who sought the region's clean, pure air and crisp, refreshing lakes.

The answer to this conundrum was the extension of a railroad line. Up to this point, the northernmost stretch of the Michigan Central Railroad had been Gaylord, some fifty miles to the south. In 1881, however, the Jackson, Lansing and Saginaw Branch of the Michigan Central completed a line running from Gaylord to Cheboygan. The following year, service was extended to Mackinaw City, fifteen miles to the north. Finally the tip of the Lower Peninsula was linked to the rest of the state and the country.[1] While clearly a milestone in the development of northern Michigan, it cannot be underestimated just how important the railroad linkage was. From Cheboygan, the Michigan Central rumbled along a railroad line which ran almost vertically through the state until it got to Grayling. From here, it went to Bay City and spurs then shot off either eastward to Detroit or westward to Chicago.[2]

From either one of these places, timber cut in Cheboygan could be sent by train all across the nation. This new medium of transport, combined with the services shipping already provided, caused a major hurdle to be cleared as far as movement of goods was concerned.

An interesting side effect of the development of railroad lines are the subsequent settlements they allow to exist. After the Michigan Central completed its new lines in Cheboygan County, a number of small towns popped up. It should be noted, however, that use of the term "town" should not infer a community with a bustling business district. Often these places were merely stops along the great iron horse's laborious trek, perhaps a lumber camp or a centralized meeting point for residents living in the area. Less frequently these little stops would be graced with the presence of a post office, though this was comparably rare. The following settlements are all those which are known to have existed along the Michigan Central's route in Cheboygan County. Some of them certainly still exist, some exist in name only, and others no longer exist at all. The communities, from north to south, were Mackinaw City, Freedom, Lake Side, Cheboygan, Mullet Lake, Bushville, Topinabee, Columbus Beach, Indian River, Hamby, Rondo, Haakwood, Wolverine, and Trowbridge; existing off the main line but still connected to the road were Afton, Taft, Armstrong, Smith's Mill, Gilchrist, Youngs, Steinhof, and Cornwell.[3]

The next major train line to the Cheboygan area did not come until 1904, with the extension of the Detroit & Mackinac.[4] Understandably it arrived with comparably less fanfare, not being "the first," but was particularly important because it put the north in direct contact with the east side of the state, instead of the central regions as with the Michigan Central. At any rate, the Detroit & Mackinac shared the Michigan Central's knack for causing little settlements to pop up. Along the former's lines the settlements were Cheboygan, Inverness, Aloha, Waveland, Churchill, Millers, Legrand, La Grand, Tower, Onaway, Sand Pit, Wolverine Switch, and Milliken.[5]

Although the Michigan Central and the Detroit & Mackinac were certainly the most important railroads in the area at this time, they were not the only ones. Lines such as these were useful in the fact that once lumber was loaded onto them, it could literally wind up anywhere in the

First arrival of the Detroit & Mackinac Railroad into Cheboygan, 1904 (Image courtesy Ellis Olson).

country. They made it easy to get wood out of lumber towns like Cheboygan and get it to market, wherever it may be. The problem still existed, though, of getting that wood out of the forest, long before it got anywhere near the mills or big cities. Getting the lumber out could be a major problem, especially if there was not adequate snowfall or cold enough temperatures to make ice on logging roads. This problem led to the development of another, more specialized type of railroad – the logging road.

The winter of 1877-78 was a particularly arduous one for lumbermen all throughout Michigan. Lack of both snow and cold temperatures made it next to impossible to get felled wood out of the forest. If the logs could not be hauled directly to a mill or body of water (to be floated to the mills), the mills would not run, and the result would be economic ruin for a good many lumber barons. The solution was to develop a railroad especially tailored for lumber which could run right from the mill to the woods or woods to river. There would be no need to haul the wood along a tote road to a stream, river or lake, as the wood only had to make it to the nearby tracks. As long as the terrain was relatively cooperative, a small narrow-gauge logging railroad could be built right up to the place of the current logging operation. They were expensive to build, but they also had plenty of benefits. Not only could they be built right to the camp site, but they could also be operated year-round, regardless of temperature or condition of a tote road. This would allow the mills to operate year-round as well, and in turn, yield more lumber *per annum* than otherwise would have been possible.

The development of the logging railroad was the greatest innovation to hit the Michigan lumber industry. The very earliest logging railroads, if they can be called such, had appeared in Michigan as early as 1850. These primitive systems consisted of horse-drawn cars running on wooden rails. But within a few years more standard roads developed, and by 1877 better than fifteen were in operation in the state; after the poor weather conditions of 1877-78, their use was greatly expanded.[6] Depending on their location, these roads either tied into other mainline roads (such the Michigan Central or Detroit & Mackinac), or were free-standing, existing solely for particular, localized operations. In the end, some five hundred logging roads existed at one time or another throughout the state.[7]

For those companies which could afford it, the logging train was clearly the way to go. As a direct result of the exceedingly temperate winter of 1877-78, lumbermen were forced to find some means of hauling timber out of the woods other than hauling it on iced-over tote roads. The McArthur, Smith & Co. did not yet have a railroad and were forced into a difficult position. Therefore, they had no other choice but to build "cars and…tracks for the purpose of drawing their logs left in the woods for want of snow" in the first part of 1878, trying to make up for the lack of other means of log transport.[8] Their railroad ran from the mill in Cheboygan to their camps in the woods. A cheaper alternative to running from camp to mill was to run from the camp to a body of water. The Thompson Smith Company chose to go this route at nearly the same time as the McArthur, Smith & Co. was building their road.[9] Due to the size of his enterprises, it would have meant certain financial doom for Smith if he had not been able to keep the Big Mill operational.

Had that mill folded, it would have caused untold hardship for not only Smith, but for Duncan City as well, his mill being the lifeblood of that community.

While railroad lines were being put down, it was becoming increasingly necessary that another type of line was also going to have to be laid in Cheboygan – water. The year after the completion of the railroad line in 1881, the Cheboygan Municipal Waterworks was constructed. The building, measuring forty by sixty feet, circulated water throughout the city via a steam driven pumping device. This machine was both costly and inefficient, although it was not replaced until decades later. At any rate, the new system was first tested and deemed acceptable on 9 September 1882. It cost the Village of Cheboygan $26,240.65 to install, but without question was well worth the expense. With the new mains in place, Cheboygan became a much more livable place, bringing in that many more prospective business and professional people, now that the downtown could better support them.[10]

Water alone is not enough to make something grow – light is needed, too. An extensive and reliable system of streetlights would provide for this. Although oil streetlamps had been in place since 1876, they were unreliable on windy nights and not particularly bright. The novelty of the electric light was first seen in Cheboygan in 1884, courtesy of the W. & A. McArthur Company. The company's electric plant was small and its primary focus was for lighting the Watermill Store the company operated at the corner of Main and Seymour Streets. The lights, proving to be the "marvel of the community," were so well liked that in 1888 the village council approved a motion to illuminate Cheboygan with electricity. The new luminous curiosity was first installed along Main Street but gradually spread outward.[11] The city now had not only plenty of water, but also lots of light to help it grow. And grow it did.

The blossoming of downtown Cheboygan as a business and commercial center was becoming more and more evident literally every year. Main Street, despite its importance to the community, was a dirt road until 1886. In the summer of that year, cedar blocks cut locally and measuring about six by six inches each side and eighteen inches high were laid along Main Street at a cost of $19,456.79. This was the first of three major improvements to Cheboygan's central artery. The cedar blocks were removed and replaced with brick in 1906, and later the thoroughfare was widened and cemented in 1926.[12]

With the completion of these noteworthy milestones, downtown developments had propelled the village to a more complete stage of refinement. During the 1880s Cheboygan had been watered, electrified, and paved, making it very attractive as a community to either settle in or establish a business. But on the other hand, now noticeably absent from such rapid growth was the smaller settlement at Duncan City. Unquestionably, Cheboygan's sister city was still an important community. The Big Mill located there produced more lumber than several of Cheboygan's mills combined. But be that as it may, the fact that the majority of the regional growth had been relegated to Cheboygan since the dredging of the river meant that any potential augmentation in Duncan City was that much less likely. Consider, for example, all that was taking place in Cheboygan: the river dredging, the extension of the railroad line, gas and electric illumination, and the paving of the downtown, and it becomes evident just what was taking place. One of two things was going to have to happen; either Cheboygan and Duncan City were going to merge into one larger city, or the latter would eventually die out from the lack of facilities and conveniences her bigger sister offered.

The emerging soon-to-be city was naturally attracting persons of all the necessary professions required for the long and short-term success of a community. Some of the more prominent figures included W.S. Humphrey, "An Attorney at Law [who] has been located in Cheboygan some four years, and in addition to his profession, is largely interested in pine and farming lands in Northern Michigan. Mr. Humphrey is a reliable business man and has contributed largely to the general prosperity of Cheboygan." There was also Mr. Porter M. Lathrop, who "located in Cheboygan last spring and is now doing a very extensive trade. He keeps a large assortment of dry goods, ladies' fancy goods, carpets, groceries, and c., which he sells at the very lowest prices." In Duncan City, J.N. Perry advertised that "Box Stoves, Sugar Kettles, Ploughs and Scrapers, will be kept constantly on hand." Hotels were aplenty in Cheboygan as well, including Mr. A. Earl's Everett House (who advertised that his hotel had "recently been enlarged and generally improved, and is now the Largest Hotel in Cheboygan. Special Inducements to Traveling Agents, Week and Day Boarders"), and M.A Gagnon's Benton House. Not all of the business owners were men, however – Mrs. S.A. Smart, proprietress of the Fountain House, "...knows well how to keep a hotel and provides well for the wants of her guests. Invalids who come north to spend the season will find a good home."[13] The presence of all these people sheds light onto the kind of growth occurring and what kind of business was going on – the business of everyday life, reflective of the fact that this emerging town was not going to be some boomtown one day and a ghost town the next.

Lumber alone did not cause all of the interest in Cheboygan. The village's first physician and an active community member, Dr. Arthur M. Gerow, made the case that his home was much more than a random sprung-up lumbering hot spot. Rather, there were other natural benefits of the area to take advantage of and enjoy. He maintained that Cheboygan had a climate which was "especially adapted" for the relief of hay fever, consumption, asthma, and dyspepsia, among other ailments. For those suffering from "general debility," Dr. Gerow said that "...the pure bracing atmosphere and the equable temperature give them a new lease of life, and inspire them with hopes to which they have long been strangers." He cites the "mildness of temperature" and "freedom from malarious diseases" as further indication of Cheboygan's agreeable climate.[14] But the good doctor failed to note the region's long and bitterly cold winters, as well as the copious amounts of snow which fall each year. In any event, people continued to come north, but more for lumbering and employment opportunities and less for medicinal reasons.

Dr. Gerow did more than just talk about how nice he thought Cheboygan was. A leader and advocate of the place, Gerow did much to help Cheboygan grow in its early days. A native of Trenton, Ontario, Gerow came to Cheboygan in 1869. He worked in a drug store before opening up an office and drug store of his own. Despite a brief departure for the west coast, Gerow made Cheboygan his home for most of the rest of his life. He built several prominent buildings in town, including an entire business block and the building once occupied by the Ottawa Hotel. He also had a pivotal part to play in the development of one of Cheboygan's lesser-known industries – fruit production. Gerow, a man of diverse interests, was responsible for the establishment of the Orchard Beach and Riverside Orchards on the outskirts of town.[15] Gerow was a man who had an integral part to play in many different phases of Cheboygan's development.

Worthy and noble citizens are the lifeblood of any community. Those who seek to do anything to the contrary are, of course, generally not welcome. Never in Cheboygan's history has there been a better example of this than in a bizarre incident which occurred in June of 1883. In what can only be described as an application of frontier justice, the people of Cheboygan knew evil when they saw it – and took the matter into their own hands.[16]

Tuesday, 12 June 1883, started as did any other day in Cheboygan. It was prime cutting season for the mills, and plenty of workingmen could be found wandering about. The village was bustling with activity as it was most everyday. The weather was pleasant and it was a fine time to be in town. About five-thirty that evening, seven-year-old Nettie Lyons wandered outside her home and went about searching for her father. Not far away, on Main Street, a man approached her and asked where she was going. She replied that she was in search of her father. The stranger reportedly said to her in reply, "Come with me, sissy, and I will show you where your papa is, he is up this way." In his devilish demeanor, he convinced the young Nettie to follow him into a swampy area just beyond the nearby railroad tracks, near the corner of Nelson and Horne Streets. Here he committed the most heinous acts imaginable. The wicked villain raped the innocent child, then in an effort to cover up his unjustifiable acts, struck her on the back of the head and stabbed her, leaving her for dead.[17]

But young Nettie was more resilient than her violator had planned. After a feverous search conducted by the entire community, the wounded child was found about five o'clock Wednesday morning. Alive but enduring unimaginable suffering, the brave youngster was able to provide a description of her attacker. Immediately a search began, involving more people than perhaps any other event in all of

Cheboygan's history. The story gained attention throughout the state, as the *Detroit Free Press* picked up the story and provided a brief synopsis in its Thursday edition. According to the *Free Press*, the assailant, if ever caught, would be in a tough predicament. "Lynching is freely talked of, and if the man is caught he will probably be disposed of with little ceremony...."[18] If only the editors knew what incredible ceremony was about to transpire.

The local paper reported that, "Men were sick at heart, business was left, and the only business was the all important business of securing the outlaw whose identity had been clearly set forth by the simple words of the crushed victim." That evening, about twelve hours after Nettie was found, a Mackinaw City lawman brought a prisoner who was potentially the offender. His name was Tillot Comstock Warner. A thirty-two year old drifter who took odd jobs where he could, he had recently wandered into town from nearby Alpena.[19] It would have been better for him had he never set foot in Cheboygan.

The community discussed nothing else that night as Warner remained locked up at the County Jail. Everyone in the village was questioning themselves and each other as to the possible guilt of this vagabond. There can be no question that everybody wanted to punish the guilty person, whoever he was. The next day the fervor continued as the community members continued their deliberations. The poor child, meanwhile, gave an accurate description of her aggressor; she cried when she saw him again. The physical evidence on Warner – a pin removed from Nettie's pants – was all the more proof of his guilt. Blood was also found on Warner's pants, and eyewitness testimony further sealed his fate. An interview by the *Northern Tribune* showed that Warner was unable to give an accurate account of his whereabouts at the time of the horrific crime. Thursday night a meeting was held at the town hall, where it was decided to wait until an examination had been undertaken to determine Warner's fate. The *Detroit Free Press* predicted that, "unless he can then by proof change the feeling it is the general opinion that Saturday's sun will find him dangling as a punishment to him and a warning to that character of men."[20] From a preliminary standpoint, he appeared guilty. Still, he was not even formally arraigned and already the community as judge, jury and soon-to-be executioner had made up its mind. Warner was guilty.

As the accused sat in his cell at the jailhouse, men across Cheboygan discussed what should be done. Citizens acknowledged the awful reality and conceded that there was no punishment on the that books would fit this disgusting crime. Discussion soon led to planning.

> Beer and whisky had nothing to say in the matter, but serious men, thinking of the supreme importance of protecting the virtue and safety of mother, wife and daughter, and also of preserving the majesty of the law, were carried as it were to an irresistible conclusion that it was their solemn duty to see the guilty suffer death.[21]

The people had spoken and were about to carry out "what ought not to be done while there is a shadow of a doubt as to the guilt of the offender...." Just a few hours after the community meeting, and without a chance for Warner to have any sort of trial, men began to assemble to mete out justice. By one o'clock Friday morning a crowd of reportedly more than a thousand had gathered outside the county jail. It was quiet, as everyone knew what was about to happen, although no one was proud of it. Despite Sheriff Harrington's efforts to prevent the inevitable, the crowd burst in and struggled for half an hour to open the main door to the detention area. They finally knocked it down, and after fumbling among the restrained lawmen for the right key to open Warner's cell, found it and hauled the accused out into the street. Unknown masked men led the calm and collected Warner not a hundred yards to the nearby railroad tracks on the aptly named Court Street. As they walked the executioners put a rope around his neck and turned to him and said, "Come on, we will show you the way to your papa, he is up this way." The defendant flinched not his face as he was led to his fate.[22]

The procession stopped at a railroad crossing sign on the side of the tracks nearest Main Street. The rope was thrown around a railroad crossing sign, and Warner was asked if he had anything to say. He protested his innocence, and then said, "The only prayer I have to make is that God will have mercy on your souls, this is all I have to say. I am innocent, and when you have hung me, probably you will find the man." The leader of the masked men then ordered Warner strung up; he was suspended by the neck from the sign, and was lowered about a minute later. In the confusion of the heated moment, he mumbled what sounded like a confession and an outcry from the people could be heard. Then he said that he was innocent again, and he was suspended for a final time. Tillot Comstock Warner was hanged from the railroad crossing sign and expired at 1:50 A.M., Friday, 16 June 1883. The body hung until night watchman Paquette found it suspended from the sign about four o'clock that morning.[23]

The brutal act of rape and attempted murder had been punished by those who had determined that no punishment was applicable to fit the crime save the most brutal death. There apparently was no law in Michigan which the citizens of Cheboygan thought would be germane to the awful transgressions committed by Warner. Although no one liked the idea of a lynch mob, it was only such an assemblage which was capable of meting out the just punishment, as far as the locals were concerned. Their opinion was not relegated to just their community, however. The *St. Ignace Republican* expressed its consent: "Well done, Cheboygan men! The world will honor you for your manliness, though some may condemn. If ever a man swung for a dastardly crime, the one you strung up deserved his fate and hell's portion beside." The *Bay City Tribune* presented its opinion on what was the greater issue and root cause of the lynching. "There is no lynching in England because crime is punished by the courts with the certainty of conviction, and there exists no need of a resort to personal vengeance. There would be no lynching in the United States if the courts performed their offices with the same reliability."[24] In sum, the lynching of Till Warner was the result of anger and hatred for a man who had committed an unthinkable act. Those who executed him, and those who watched him hang with delight, vocalized and ultimately actualized their frustrations in the most horrible and dramatic way – taking the law into their own hands.

The hanging immediately made front-page news in the *Detroit Free Press*. It was a very serious event which brought up debate about vigilante justice and lynch law throughout the state. An incident like this also causes many questions to be raised regarding guilt or innocence. The *Free Press* reported that at least some people, including Joe Littlefield, the man who brought Warner into town, expressed serious doubt about his guilt. What is more, the lawmen in charge of guarding him were accused of "merely formal resistance" to the lynch mob.[25] Whatever the case may be, it can hardly be said that Warner received any sort of justice. The whole incident, carried about by emotional fervor and contempt, led to the brutal execution of a man without the right of a trial. There is no indication that the search for the perpetrator continued after Warner was brought before the citizens of Cheboygan, nor were those who lynched him ever brought to trial themselves. The official verdict on the lynching of Till Warner was "Came to his death at the hands of unknown parties."[26]

Was Tillot Comstock Warner guilty of the crimes with which he was charged? Looking at the information which has been reported and taking into account Warner's own testimony, a casual glance at the facts would yield an answer in the affirmative. There is no reason to believe that Warner was not the guilty party based on available evidence. Other questions must be addressed, however. Was the local fervor and pomp surrounding the incident a catalyst leading to a lynching that, apparently, was in the works even before a suspect was apprehended? Despite the assertions that "Beer and whiskey had nothing to say in the matter," was this in fact partly to blame? Warner was lynched at about one o'clock in the morning – high time to be on the way home from the saloon. Whatever the case may be, the lynching of Till Warner was highly unusual not only for Cheboygan but for Michigan as a whole. It was an isolated incident of the application of quick justice from a frontier community. Unfortunate though the entire event was, it should be noted that such occurrences were not unprecedented in remote regions, despite the fact that Michigan had already been a state for several decades. There is no easy explanation for what happened. As communities grew and expanded during the late nineteenth century, sometimes things happened (as they do today) that are difficult to explain. In a period of formation and development, an awful event occurred which was the result of a desire for justice and the removal of pestilence from a growing community. With growth occurring and the people of Cheboygan willing to show their desire for righteousness in their town in such an extreme way, any potential villain would think twice before doing his dirty work in Cheboygan.

Thankfully, more permanent and beneficial things were occurring in Cheboygan at this time as well. While there was by now plenty of people and capital flowing into the area, it still needed a reliable financial institution. It is in light of this fact that Cheboygan's most prominent early bank, the First National Bank of Cheboygan, was born. The predecessor to this bank existed long before its eventual incorporation. The First National Bank's predecessor and the first organized banking institution in the city was the private bank operated by G.D.V. Rollo. He, and W.F. De Puy working with him, opened a banking institution in the spring of 1875. In 1878 De Puy sold out, and the name was changed to Rollo and Hitchcock.[27] In 1882, upon the advice of his doctor, Rollo, by this time a well-respected man in the community, left Cheboygan for a more suitable climate, and so he and Hitchcock both sold out their interests. The bank was bought by William McArthur, George F. Reynolds, John W. McGinn, Jacob J. Post, and T.T. Van Arsdale. The new institution became known as The Cheboygan Banking Company of Wm. McArthur and Co.[28]

From this, in 1882 the First National Bank of Cheboygan was organized. It was given its federal charter on 6 August 1884 with John W. McGinn as president and George F. Reynolds as cashier.[29] Its starting capital was $50,000, a modest sum for the creation of a bank at the time, but still no less respectable. The bank became for many years a strong and stable financial bastion in the community. In 1883-84 an impressive new bank was built at the corner of Main and Division Streets which became a visible manifestation of the strong foundation the bank provided for the community. By 1887 the financial resources of the bank had grown and had in surplus $2,500, and by about 1900 showed one of $10,000.[30] In a time of expansion and growth, a fine institution had been established to provide for the needs of the community for many years to come.

The First National Bank was not the only bank in Cheboygan, however. A bank operated by H.A. Wetmore also existed for a brief time. Very little is known about this institution, except that it was founded in 1885 and had closed its doors for unknown reasons by about 1890.[31] Two decades later, in 1905, the Cheboygan County Savings Bank was organized by local brewer James F. Moloney and lumber baron William L. Martin. Later, this bank would be bought out several times in favor of larger interests.[32]

Despite all of these numerous advances – material and financial – there were setbacks as well. Fire remained a constant threat to the city, especially considering many of the buildings were built close together and of wood. In 1886 Cheboygan's famed Opera House went up in flames, putting the building and the entire downtown in considerable danger. The fire spread to the City Hall section of the building, where a man by the name of Doggie Dumaw was being held in the village jail. With nowhere to go, Dumaw was trapped as the flames encircled him and he perished in the inferno. Luckily, the fire did not spread more than it did and was contained to the single building. Clearly a favorite with the locals (the municipal facilities notwithstanding), it did not take long for the Opera House to be rebuilt. On 30 July 1888 the Opera House was back in business, with the Browne Theatre Company putting on several productions that night, opening with *Fogg's Ferry*. Sadly, a smoldering cigarette would lead to another fire that damaged the facility again in 1903. But just as before, the resilience of Cheboygan's people would not permit her main cultural and entertainment edifice to lie in ruins. The following year, it was back in business.[33]

With the establishment of these institutions, in addition to the utilities and ease of physical transportation, the northern communities were poised both materially and economically for success. Both Duncan City with its excellent natural harbor and Cheboygan, with its now more navigable river system and good financial structure, grew to become most noteworthy lumbering communities. Population numbers reflect this rapid growth. Between 1880 and 1890, Cheboygan's population increased 175 percent (even Detroit's growth during this time was only seventy-seven percent), and the male-female ratio was improving (now eight men to seven females).[34] The growing communities were continuing their expansion as they became more settled, more organized, and more essential to the rest of the world. The 1890s would see the peak of this growth and contribute to the economic boom that Cheboygan and Duncan City would soon enjoy.

The 1873 *History of Cheboygan and Mackinac Counties – Business and Manufacturing Statistics, Soil, Timber, Prospects for Settlers, and c.* predicted that "...from every indication at the present time, this point must in the future be the leading commercial city of the Straits, and within five years we expect to see Cheboygan an incorporated city with a population from 5,000 to 7,000 inhabitants, with largely increased manufacturing and commercial facilities."[35] This prediction was not too far off. On 13 March 1889 the Michigan's legislature approved the incorporation of the City of Cheboygan.[36] As the 1890s began, Cheboygan was well posed for future success. The foundation had been laid and the solid mortar of men, material and money had all led to the building of a very solid foundation.

4

Unprecedented Prosperity

The Cheboygan that had emerged from the 1880s had shown fantastic growth. The increase of the city, be it in size or modern convinces, had dramatically transformed an area that just four decades prior was little more than a couple of cabins. Duncan City should not be ignored either, for although most of the steady growth was in Cheboygan, the former had seen its fair share of development too. In both cases, now booming communities existed and local businessmen talked of the unquestionably bright future that the settlements had. Even after the lumber boom, they assured themselves, Cheboygan would continue to be an economically thriving area with continued prosperity. For the moment, there was little reason to think otherwise.

A look at downtown Cheboygan circa 1890 exhibits every sign of a thriving community. Along Main Street were multiple grocers, drug stores, jewelers, a butcher, photographer, dentist, cigar factory, and even a steam laundry facility. All of this is in addition to the many hotels which had sprung up – including the Cass, Benton, and New Cheboygan, all three of which were located on the corner of Third (now State) and Water Street. And, like most good frontier towns, there was an abundance of saloons to frequent if a lumberman found himself thirsty. Between Third Street and Elm Street alone, a distance of a mere four blocks, there were no fewer than five saloons. And in the two-block distance between Main Street and the river, along Third Street, there were six.[1]

Amongst the saloons and grocers there were plenty of other establishments reflective of daily life as well. Dwellings, doctor's offices, newspaper printing facilities, drug stores, the City Hall and Opera House and banks all contributed to what must have been quite the lively downtown. There could be no doubt in 1890 Cheboygan that things were heading in the right direction.[2] It was an exciting place to be, full of promise and hope for the future.

Despite their distance apart, as time went on Cheboygan and Duncan City were gradually becoming more and more integrated. Although Jeremiah Duncan had built a connecting road between the two communities four decades prior, it was still a considerable distance to travel on foot. A clever solution was devised in the form of a horse-drawn street car. In 1893 D.J. Kennedy, from Bay City, Michigan, opened up Cheboygan's first (and only) mass-transit system. Initially the small system carried citizens just around Cheboygan and the Michigan Central Railroad depot, but it did not take long before Kennedy extended the line to Duncan City. For a nickel, a person in need of a ride could go between Cheboygan and her sister city or vice versa. A total of three cars made up the Cheboygan-Duncan City transit line.[3]

While the system worked fine in the summer, the operation of such a line was exceedingly difficult in a place known for its brutal winters. Frequent heavy snowfall would quickly bury street car rails, and uncovering them would not have been an effective use of anyone's time or money. The solution was to forgo the tracks and wheels and instead use skis. In winter, the cars were taken off their wheels and mounted on runners and heated by a stove, "a method of transportation visible nowhere else in this broad land save in our city." Without the limitations of rails, trolley trips went as far out of town as the Tannery on Cheboygan's south end.[4]

After only three years in operation, however, Kennedy's street car business began to feel the pinch. The cars stopped running in 1896 but were put back into service in 1898 when another entrepreneur named Charles Howell tried his hand at the business. Sadly, that year was also the year in which a great tragedy in Duncan City destroyed not only the town's most important employer, but also the future of the Cheboygan – Duncan City line. The trolley system was promptly abandoned and the tracks all pulled up. The cars themselves were sold to be used as play houses for children.[5] A fascinating story in Cheboygan's history, the street car system did not last long. Other aspects of the growth of this period had much more lasting consequences.

In line with the growth of the communities, church development followed in kind during the 1890s. The swelling faithful met their needs for spiritual satisfaction through any one of a number of churches, the largest being St. Mary's Roman Catholic Parish. One description of Cheboygan in the 1890s explains: "Membership is increasing in all of the churches. The Catholic church has so many members and serves so many people who speak very little, if any, English, that it has to have French and Polish assistants to aid in handling the work." The church of the social elite, however, was the Episcopal church, although most of the churches were in general cordial with one another. More important, however, was the assertion that "Cheboygan is well 'churched' for a lumber town."[6] This is particularly significant because it shows that even though Cheboygan was a frontier town (although gradually becoming less so), it was atypical in the sense that its residents were of a different mindset than one would typically see in such a place. Considering the seasonal, transient nature of a number of the workers in lumbering communities, one would not expect that church attendance would be that high. Perhaps this is one reason why Cheboygan remained well populated even after the lumber ran out. Its residents were already considering the permanency of their community, or at the very least seeing themselves as permanent residents. There were plenty of jobs at the moment and with Cheboygan's ideal physical location, any number of occupations or businesses could easily succeed (lumber or no lumber), or so the predominant opinion dictated.

Arguably the single most important company operating in Cheboygan at this time was the W. & A. McArthur Company. Their large mill (located at the terminus of Seymour Street, near the river) in 1895 was capable of processing 100,000 feet of wood every ten hours. The impressive facility consisted of one gang saw, two circular saws, one lathe machine, one edging table, two trimming tables and three butting saws.[7] To keep this equipment running the company occasionally ran more than five lumber camps and had as many as 300 men working in the woods at one time. In 1895 they even had some 250 men lumbering in Canada.[8] They produced an extensive array of timber products. The planing mill and lumber yard on site regularly had on hand rough and dressed lumber, flooring, ceiling, siding, moldings and building material.[9]

Two bridges went from the McArthur mill to the other side of the river. One was a red painted wooden bridge used by employees to reach their company-owned homes on the other side. The other was laid with rails and had in operation a horse-drawn car which carried sawdust to be deposited in a giant mound on the other side. The McArthur Company had little choice in the erection of this bridge, considering they were no longer allowed to deposit their sawdust into the river. This gigantic pile, once billed as the greatest sawdust pile in the world (at about 150 feet high), stood for nearly a century as a very visible remnant of the immense size of the McArthur operations. Because it was essentially ever-growing, it would occasionally be burned to reduce its size. Needless to say, not everyone in the community was appreciative of this process.

> The company deliberately set the pile on fire every winter to keep it from becoming too large. The clouds of smoke ruined many a family washing. Angry housewives finally got together and registered a vehement complaint which caused the City Council to prohibit setting fire to the pile.[10]

Despite numerous attempts to find a useful application of the pile after the closing of the mill, nothing practical could be found. Caverns had formed in the mound which playing children could easily fall into. The pile was also known to spontaneously catch fire from time to time, posing yet another safety issue. With a bit of sadness, "The World's Largest Sawdust Pile" was finally trucked away in 2000. Rumors that visiting circus elephants had inadvertently fallen into the pile and became encapsulated in the mess were, not surprisingly, proven to be nothing more than unsubstantiated legend.

What set the McArthur Company apart are the additional goods that they produced other than lumber (and a big sawdust pile). Beginning in 1869, the old shingle mill at the site near the river dam was converted for use as a grist and flour mill.[11] By the same time the lumber mill was processing all its timber in 1895, the flour mill located on the same site could produce 125 barrels of flour per twenty-four hours. Three water driven wheels produced 175 horsepower of electricity to drive the reels and separators necessary for the production of wheat flour.[12]

The variety of flour the McArthur Company produced was quite extensive. The flour making division of the company was known as the Cheboygan Roller Mills. Rivaling the diversity of their lumber-producing ventures, the company turned out numerous types of flours: Diamond (Fancy Patent), Peerless (Patent), Extra Baker's, and Northern Belle. They also manufactured graham, whole wheat, rye, and buckwheat flours, in addition to bolted and granulated corn meal and grain and mill feeds.[13] After producing this impressive variety of flour and feed, the products would then find their way into the company store (open to the public) or be sent to some other destination. The locally produced merchandise could then be sold locally or shipped to any number of faraway destinations. As one historian has suggested, "It would appear that the flour mill was most successful and that profit from the lumbering activity made the venture possible."[14] Indeed, both the lumber mill and the Cheboygan Roller Mills were important businesses in Cheboygan, extant because of the lumber industry.

The McArthur Company did not stop at merely manufacturing lumber and flour. They opened one of the first retail lumber outlets in 1883, but would end up becoming retail dealers in much more.[15] An ad from their very-well outfitted department store claimed that, "You cannot fail to find exactly what you want by looking over our complete stock." This may very well have been true. The Watermill Store offered hardware, china, cooking vessels, a large variety of dried fruits and nuts, candy, potatoes, cream cheese, a variety of meats, and, of course, flour, to name just a few items. In the mid-nineties, three pounds of tea could be had for a dollar, six pounds of crackers for a quarter, light pork for six cents per pound, and twenty-two pounds of sugar for a dollar.[16] The Watermill Store was one of the largest in northern Michigan. It was made up of three departments; grocery, dry goods, and crockery and hardware.[17]

Once the lumber had been cut at the McArthur lumber mill, it was then hauled to the mouth of the Cheboygan River to the company docks, a distance of about a mile and a half. Lumber was then stored there as it awaited shipping or delivery. These docks served other purposes as well. Additional McArthur Company goods such as hard and soft coal, brick, lime, cement, and salt were kept at or near the warehouses at the docks for sale locally or far away.[18] A popular steamship destination for many tourists and vacationers, incoming passengers on lake-going ships from around the Midwest tied up at the McArthur docks. A number of passenger lines called at the docks, including the Detroit & Cleveland, Hart Line, Northern Michigan Line, People's Line, and the Arnold Line. These routes connected Cheboygan with many places around the state and the nation. Sault Ste. Marie, St. Ignace, Mackinac Island, Cheboygan and Detroit were all interlinked within Michigan, and Green Bay, Wisconsin, Sandusky, Ohio and Chicago outside the state.[19] As the boats were about to dock at Cheboygan, arriving visitors would often throw pennies off the ship and into the water. Local children would jump in after them, unquestionably a number of which would end up being spent in McArthur's Watermill Store.

From the diversified interests of the W. & A. McArthur Company, it is clear that they succeeded in a number of sectors in the local market. So large and economically significant was the company that it even issued its own scrip between pay days, in denominations of five, ten, twenty-five, and fifty cents and one and two dollars, redeemable at the company store and then deducted from forthcoming wages.[20] The McArthur Company was an impressive exemplar of what lumber could do to a community. It must be remembered that this is the reason any of these ventures started to begin with. Lumber was crucially important. Had the McArthur Company not gotten involved with the purchase of the Duncan estate, they would not have been providing lumber or cured citron and fancy large raisins at their store to the residents of northern Michigan.

Even though there clearly were other occupations in Cheboygan other than lumbering, it is because of lumbering that those other jobs even existed in the first place. Virtually everyone who worked in Cheboygan either did something directly related to lumbering or provided services to those working in the industry.[21] Because of the rapid construction of buildings in the United States, people needed lumber – and the city of Cheboygan in the 1890s could easily provide for such a demand. Within Cheboygan at this time were nine sawmills and two shingle mills – and total annual production of sawed lumber was more than 100 million board feet. By 1896, the total output of lumber for the county would be double that number.[22]

Further evidence of the boom of this period is presented in an 1893 book issued by the State of Michigan entitled *Michigan and its Resources*. A section on Cheboygan County describes the city: "Cheboygan, a rapidly growing town of 7,000 inhabitants, is the county seat. It is a live port, with all modern improvements, sewers, paved streets, street cars, electric lights, $40,000 opera house, splendid schools and churches."[23] Where just a few decades ago were nothing but trees and a quiet, shallow river, now were multiple sawmills, businesses, churches, and, essential to it all, a growing population.

Responsibility for the growth unquestionably lies in what Cheboygan was producing. A snippet from the *Cheboygan Democrat* gives an excellent glimpse into the booming city's output. From the 8 December 1894 edition:

> For the month of November, 17,896,000 feet of lumber was shipped from this port, making 102,756,000 feet for the season. This is several million feet more than was cut during the [last] season, and there cannot be as heavy stock on the docks as last fall. The other shipments were 1,370,000 lath, 2,727,000 shingles, 6,500 ties, 17,000 posts, 612 bushels potatoes, 204 tons flour, 1,084 tons merchandise, and 700 telegraph poles. The receipts were, 98 cords wood, 9 tons salt, 232 barrels cement, 6,000 bushels grain, 475 tons feed, 169 packages fruit, 19 head stock, 694 tons flour, 1,300 tons coal, 184 tons hay and 2,204 tons merchandise.

Cheboygan was producing a great amount of material not only for consumption locally but elsewhere as well. Naturally lumber tops the list of local exports, but the presence of items like flour and potatoes are noteworthy as well. Additionally, the fact that material and finished goods ready for market were coming in at the same time as they were going out showed that Cheboygan had the necessary wherewithal to be not only an export community, but a place of general commercial trade as well.

Downtown Cheboygan, circa 1895, had grown considerably compared to the same area five years prior. With the population now near 7,000, there was even greater need for the everyday necessities of life. In places where before there was empty space now stood new tailors, liveries, a foundry, a shingle mill and yard, and, of course, dwellings. Literally thousands of people were coming to the Cheboygan area to be part of the lumber boom.[24]

This rapid growth naturally begs the question, who are all these people coming to Cheboygan? Generally speaking, many of them came from the western sections of the northeastern states, such as New York and Pennsylvania. Many of the people who moved here to take part in lumbering had previously done so in these locales. But large numbers of local settlers were increasingly immigrants, most notably the growing influx of Canadians who already made up near a quarter of the total Michigan population by 1869.[25] As other groups began immigrating in higher numbers, Cheboygan became a good example of the diverse society which Michigan, and the United States as a whole, was becoming.

A look at numbers from the 1890 United States Census provides some further insight. Total population for Cheboygan County at this time was 11,986. Roughly a third of these people were foreign-born – Germans, Irish, English, Poles, and Swedes were all represented to varying degrees (recall Jeremiah Duncan's hiring of an entire boatload of Swedes in the early days of settlement). No group, however, approaches the numbers of immigrants from Canada / Newfoundland. Nearly 3,000 of Cheboygan County's total inhabitants at this time were born there.[26] The peak year of lumber production, 1895, would lead one to believe that this was the year Cheboygan's population probably also peaked. This year would be the last, however, for its heyday. The fact that lumber mills were capable of producing huge amounts of product cannot be over-emphasized. The thousands of workers and their families coming to northern Michigan were doing so for a reason. Simply put, the factories needed employees (and consequently so did the rest of Cheboygan's businesses) to meet the needs of lumber manufacturing and its effects on community expansion.

The ability to produce staggering amounts of finished lumber and timber products harvested from local forests was a great economic catalyst. Other large sawmills in the community like the Cheboygan Lumber Company (predecessor to M.D. Olds & Company), Swift & Clark, and Pelton & Reid could all process tens of thousands of feet of logs daily. Despite the high capacity these mills had, (and perhaps because of it), an unfortunate reality would eventually set in. While an average log harvested in the 1860s contained some 1500 board feet of lumber, already by the 1890s harvested logs sometimes consisted of no more than sixteen board feet.[27] The situation was pretty clear – Cheboygan was eventually going to run out of what was the basis for its entire economy. The fact that there simply was not enough wood close by to maintain this rapid growth and incessant harvesting was what would eventually cause the demise of the lumber industry in the surrounding region.

The rafting of logs from Canada soon remained the only hope for saving the lumber industry in Cheboygan and Duncan City. In the complicated world of international politics, a "tit-for-tat" series of spats between the governments of the United States and the Dominion of Canada had caused the tariff situation to become detrimentally unstable between the two neighboring countries. Prior to 1890, a series of bills passed by the United States put a high duty on its exported lumber products, much of which was going to Canada. The Canadians, in retaliation, put a law in place which charged a duty of two dollars per thousand board feet (M) of logs. Because Michigan was beginning to run out of logs which American lumbermen in Michigan needed, this became a serious problem. The two dollar tariff was so high that it made the entire effort of rafting logs to the States unprofitable for most operators.[28] Michigan lumbermen, meanwhile, were becoming increasingly needful of an alternate source of logs, including operators in Cheboygan.

An agreement, if it can be called that, was struck between the two nations with the passing of the McKinley Bill in October 1890. This act abolished the duty Canadians were forced to pay, and in return they reduced their two dollar per M tariff to one dollar. But just when it appeared things were starting to improve, the Wilson Bill of 1894 eliminated the duty paid on imported Canadian lumber products, essentially creating unwanted competition for American lumbermen from this duty-free lumber. As a result, lumber organizations all across the country banded together to appeal to the government for a change in trade policy. Their cries were answered in 1897 with the passage of the Dingley Bill, which restored the two dollar duty that had previously been imposed on Canadian lumber.[29]

Not unexpectedly, the Canadians did not take too kindly to this. They also did not appreciate a spiteful proviso in the Dingley Bill that threatened an *ad valorem* tax of twenty-five percent of lumber products imported into the United States if they re-imposed any sort of export duty of their own. The Canadian response was swift and effective. In a move feared by American lumbermen, the royal government banned altogether the export of logs. No logs cut after 1 April 1898 would be permitted to be exported to the United States. With no logs being rafted from Canada, mills in the Great Lakes region, especially along Lake Huron, would be in serious trouble. What made matters worse was that a fair amount of American operators, including the W. & A. McArthur Company, had purchased land or stumpage rights to property in Canada. After the export ban, some of these lumbermen challenged the legality of the law in court. Their appeals were rejected, the Canadian government saying that the lumbermen were simply licensed to cut trees, and not guaranteed anything else. The fight went all the way to England, where the royal government had no better news for the American businessmen. This was the end of the road for many Michigan mill operators.[30] When what trees were left were exhausted, it would be time to move on farther west or to Canada, or close up shop completely. As one lumber baron put it, "Men who are brought up in the lumber business, cannot well get away from it and they go where the lumber is." Consequently, production of many mills dropped dramatically. In the case of the W. & A. McArthur Co., by 1900 production had fallen to 75,000 feet per 10 hours.[31]

In a time when the economic situation was growing ever-more complicated, a further setback occurred when the Big Mill of Thompson

Smith's Sons in Duncan City went up in flames early in the morning of Monday, 26 September 1898. Within five minutes after the fire was ignited the mill was completely engulfed. The Duncan City fire department was quickly on the scene, but their response time would likely have been faster had there been enough steam in the boilers at the mill to sound the appropriate alarm. The fire itself erupted in the shingle mill section of the facility, were there is often a great deal of dust and shavings that can quickly ignite.[32]

The exact cause of the fire may never be known, but the *Cheboygan Democrat* put forth what it thought was the "most reasonable theory:"

> The fire was at this end of the shingle mill, and when the watchman heard the crackle of the flames he ran upstairs and found only this end of the mill on fire... Empty bottles have been found at different times when cleaning up indicating that some convivial imbibers had stolen in and enjoyed themselves. The theory is that some drunken sailors had been having a quiet time and were smoking as well as drinking and the sparks from a pipe or cigar or a match dropped in the combustible dust, and the result was disastrous to a large number of people.[33]

Indeed the results were disastrous. Some 100 men lost their jobs, but this number does not take into account all of those who supported these men in Duncan City, such as merchants and street car employees. Worst of all was that the mill only carried $60,000 worth of insurance – far too little to rebuild one of the largest lumber processing facilities in the state. But going beyond a financial loss, the destruction of the Big Mill was an emotional loss as well.

> ...All day Monday groups of disconsolate men could be seen standing around viewing the ruins and apparently feeling the misfortune as greatly as the owners. Many of these men have grown up in Duncan and had never been employed by any other firm, and they felt that they had been burned out of house and home.[34]

In a certain sense, they had been burned out of house and home. With the burning of the mill and no plans to rebuild, they lost their livelihood and eventually their town. It was reported early on that, "the indications are that a new mill will be built, depending a great deal on the action of the lumber commission in Canada."[35] This statement was quixotic at best and was more than likely wishful thinking. The Canadian government had already spoken, and with much less lumber available locally, it would have made little sense economically to rebuild the mill. Thompson Smith Jr., successor to his father and proprietor of the mill, had no choice but to tell his employees that it could not be rebuilt.[36] Duncan City, which had already found itself in the precarious position of being in danger of abandonment because of the lack of facilities its sister city provided, was now dealt a fatal blow.

There were subsequent attempts to revitalize Duncan City, especially under the direction of long-time resident Egbert Smith. He attempted to start two different businesses, the Duncan Bay Manufacturing Company and the Novelty Works. Neither one of these were greeted with much success, and both soon collapsed.[37] Sadly, there was nothing left in the village to fuel its limited economy, and the Cheboygan suburb rapidly became a ghost town. The workers who formerly called it home were obliged to find jobs elsewhere.

The lack of timber, especially white pine, proved to be an irreconcilable difficulty for many of Cheboygan's mill operators. The mills still in operation in Cheboygan were forced to try to find some way to keep their mills operating. Some tried floating lumber down from the Upper Peninsula – but this was not going to last forever either.[38] Consequently, most moved out of town and headed west or north to Canada, to where new expanses of virgin timber were located, so that they could continue to make their fortunes in some other place. Local working men also had to go where work was, and when the lumber became scarcer, the lumbermen followed suit. Just as quickly as they had come to Cheboygan, they had to move on to some other booming lumber locale.

As early as 1888 the terminal disposition of the "endless" pine forests of the north was being considered. In November of that year the *Cheboygan Democrat* briefly entertained this notion.

> It is worth noting that some of the largest pine producers are turning their attention to a considerable extent to other woods than pine, which is not only an indication that they are approaching the end of their pine stumpage supply, but that they are beginning to find that their hitherto valueless hardwood trees may be marketed as lumber on a basis to make it profitable to saw them.[39]

Both statements are true. Not only was pine an exhaustible resource after all, but the lumber that was previously ignored as being worthless or a nuisance was now being seen as a potential profit generator. Oak, elm, basswood, maple, cedar, and hemlock would become important as more and more pine was harvested and eventually exhausted. Only those lumber barons and mill operators who learned to adapt to the changing market would survive in the long run. At this point in time, however, northern Michigan was in fairly good shape regarding what timber was still standing. In the southern part of the state, quality lumber was disappearing at a much faster rate, a result not only of the fact that there were more operators there, but also because lumbering in that region started decades prior to the expansion of the industry into northern Michigan.

Ten years later, the booklet *Cheboygan, Up-to-Date* (1898) acknowledged the fact that lumber was becoming less and less plentiful even in the north, but offered no reason to think that the situation was going to become any worse.

> It is estimated that there is contiguous to Cheboygan more soft wood suitable for the manufacture of paper pulp than in any other section of the United States and this, coupled with the water power and transportation facilities, means that Cheboygan will soon become famous for paper and pulp manufacture.[40]

"Famous" may have been a bit strong of a word, but Cheboygan did become a rather large paper-product manufacturing center even before the supply of pine ran out. After a long and prosperous run, in 1902 the W. & A. McArthur Company facilities were sold to the Union Paper Company, while lumber baron Millard D. Olds bought their docks at the mouth of the river.[41] The old lumber piles were all removed and the existing buildings greatly expanded. The main building was of particularly considerable size; the new length at the longest point was some 475 feet, compared to McArthur's largest of just under 150 feet.[42] Subsequently this company would become the American Pulp and Paper Company, Charmin Paper Company (of Procter and Gamble), and finally the Great Lakes Tissue Company, as it stands today.[43] So while it is true that the manufacturing of lumber and lumber products did see a very substantial decline at the beginning of the twentieth century, it did not mean that there was an abandonment of lumbering *per se*. Rather, what began to happen was an adaptation in what was produced. (M.D. Olds, for example, had a contract with the Cheboygan Paper Company to provide wood chips for fuel. In this case, lumber was both needed for fuel and for manufacture of the actual finished product, providing an advantageous situation for both companies.)[44]

Nevertheless, there were other entities in Cheboygan providing jobs other than those directly involved with lumbering. The most notable of these was the tannery of the Pfister & Vogel Leather Company, headquartered in Milwaukee, Wisconsin. Built in 1892, "the Tannery," as it became known colloquially, employed some 150 men and consisted of thirty buildings.[45] Its ultimate construction in Cheboygan was something of a bribe. A group of concerned businessmen known as the Cheboygan Improvement Association enticed a tanning company to build after at least half a dozen other firms had surveyed the area and for one reason or another decided not to build. Cheboygan was to give the new tannery owners a site and a right-of-way on a spur of track connecting it to the Michigan Central Railroad line. According to the agreement, one year after the tannery was constructed the proprietors would become the owners of the land *pro bono*.[46] A Mr. Stratton agreed to the proposal (evidently for the firm McConnell and Shaw of Boston), but three months later two gentlemen from Milwaukee, Pfister and Vogel, purchased controlling interests in the company.[47]

By December 1892 the plant was in operation, with tanning capacity at a thousand hides per day.[48] A massive enterprise covering twenty-five acres, not only did the Tannery create many jobs, it also purchased from the community fourteen to fifteen thousand cords of hemlock bark annually which was used in the tanning of hides.[49] The Tannery primarily tanned cow hides, although others could be tanned as well, should a customer desire. The process itself used hemlock bark extract which, when placed on a hide to be tanned, caused a chemical reaction which prevented decomposition of the leather. The hide was then pulled ("tawed") and oiled and finally rolled. From here it was shipped out by rail on the Michigan Central Railroad to be distributed to any number of places.[50] Pfister & Vogel had distributors in Boston, Chicago, San Francisco, New Orleans, Cincinnati, St. Louis, and St. Paul, with offices as far away as Frankfurt, Germany and London, England. It is quite possible, indeed likely, that leather tanned in Cheboygan made its way all over the world.

The Tannery itself had its own 50,000-gallon water tower, company store, apartments, hospital, and a saloon nearby. Numerous houses were built across the street for employees and their families, owned by Pfister & Vogel but rented to employees. There was even a public school next to these houses for the children.[51] The Tannery was almost a city itself, a massive complex that contributed a great deal to Cheboygan in terms of industry, employment, and financial infusion into the community.

The Tannery was also responsible for a much lesser-known chapter in Cheboygan's history. Tanners, in their handling of animal hides, are naturally more susceptible to diseases which those hides may contain. One of these diseases, though rarely encountered, is caused by infection with the highly contagious *bacillus anthracis* – anthrax. Many of the hides which were processed at the Tannery were imported, including some from China. One day a Canadian immigrant named John J. Murray was handling one of these hides. The animal to which it had once belonged was a carrier of the dreaded disease, and through some inadvertent skin-to-skin contact (or inhalation of spores from the hide), Murray contracted anthrax. A few days after being diagnosed, he succumbed to the illness and died on 4 September 1900.[52] Anthrax was extremely rare in the United States then as now, but was known to occur from time to time among those working with animal skins. So while the incident was an extremely rare occurrence, it was not completely unheard of.

Of course, there were other businesses in town which carried with them no risk of exposure to anthrax. First among these was that of the Moloney brothers and their beer. Purchased about 1881, the Northern Brewery, operated by James F. and Patrick Moloney, manufactured around forty barrels of beer per day in 1884. Theirs was a successful venture. The original facilities at the end of Court Street, along the river, had 110 feet on Main Street and was two stories high. Their storage cellar measured forty by seventy feet and was twelve feet high, "but [the Moloneys] are soon to enlarge their works in order to meet the rapidly increasing demands for their beer, which already has a wide reputation for its excellence, and is a favorite in the market." It earned much praise, especially by the United States Health Reports:

> This beer is absolutely devoid of the slightest trace of adulteration, but, upon the other hand is composed of the best of malt and choicest of hops. Its tonic qualities are of the highest and it can be used with the greatest benefit and satisfaction by old and young. Its use can conscientiously be prescribed by the physician with the certainty that a better, purer or more wholesome beverage could not possibly be found.[53]

With a compliment like that, it is no wonder the Moloneys did so well. They sold their different brews under the labels of Silvo and High Grade Export. Previous to opening the brewery the brothers had operated a grocery store in addition to other interests, both locally and in at least one other Michigan community.[54] The brothers did very well for themselves, with James Moloney becoming Cheboygan's first mayor in 1889. He was re-elected in 1896 and 1897, before going on to pursue other interests in the community.[55]

An additional industry that was extremely important to Cheboygan was that of fishing. Situated on Lake Huron and connected to a number of inland streams, rivers, and lakes, Cheboygan was an ideal spot for harvesting the waterways' resources. As early as 1884 one individual alone shipped 364,850 pounds of fish from the town during a two month period.[56] Later, packing plants owned by men with the names of Booth, Eddy, Shawl, Bell and Robbins would all contribute greatly to the local economy, especially later on as the lumber industry waned.[57] By 1912, annual harvests of fish produced around 150,000 boxes, valued at the time at approximately $100,000.[58] Thus, even though lumbering was unquestionably the most important industry in Cheboygan and the one most responsible for its growth, it was not the only one. Each and every business and industry, regardless of its size, all had an important part to play in Cheboygan's economy.

Perhaps less known but no less important is the interesting role Cheboygan had in the development of the snow plow. Brutal northern Michigan winters necessitated that the area's roads be kept clear and passable, not only for general traffic, but for another type of traffic as well – moving sleighs of lumber. Tote roads were essential to the movement of freshly cut trees, and they absolutely had to be kept clear and compacted so that the horses (or later caterpillar locomotives) could make their way through the woods and to their destination. In 1890 P.B. Brazel of the Bradford Brazel Company of Cheboygan patented a snow plow capable of keeping roads, especially logging roads, clear of snow.[59] Designed to be pulled by horses, the Brazel Plow essentially consisted of an A-shaped sleigh with large metal blades on the front to push away the snow and cut out a usable path. Brazel, who billed his product as "The only snow plow of actual merit," produced several different varieties, including the Lumbermen's Plow, a specially designed model for clearing logging roads. This machine could be equipped with a rut cutter to make it even easier for the log carrying sleighs to use the road. Brazel's plows were very popular regionally, and were even sold as far away as Washington state. Initially manufactured by Thompson Smith's Sons in Duncan City, in 1920 Schwartz Boiler Works of Cheboygan took over the patent, and continued manufacturing plows until the growing popularity of the motorized vehicle rendered the Brazel plow antiquated.[60]

One story bordering on the bizarre is Cheboygan's very short lived auto industry. Organized about 1914 in Chicago by Elias S. Flagler, the Flagler Cyclecar Company decided shortly after its establishment to base its operations in Cheboygan. Flagler and his associates then went there to drum up support for their automobile and to attempt to secure investments from local community members. Flagler built an automobile and a half in an old factory within the course of a day to show the local businessmen the speed with which one could be made. Impressed with what they saw, many (including Dr. A.M. Gerow) then put up sizeable amounts of cash to fund this new local industry.[61]

The car which was built was quite the machine indeed. It was equipped with a four-cylinder Perkins engine, side-by-side seating, and had a wheelbase of ninety inches. Advertisements proclaimed "54 Miles at 40 Miles Speed on One Gallon of Gasoline."[62] This was, perhaps, too good to be true. No more Flaglers were ever made in Cheboygan. After the would-be industrialists got their money from the community, they drove away in the vehicle they had just made and were never seen again.[63] This strange chapter in Cheboygan's history is also her only venture into automobile manufacturing. Had the Flagler Cyclecar Company been run by more honorable businessmen, perhaps the story of large-scale manufacturing in Cheboygan would have been a lot different; but because of their dishonesty, it was indeed better for them to have left town, otherwise they would have made an appearance in one of the downtown's newest and most beautiful buildings.

Cheboygan, as the seat of the county, was therefore the seat of government for the region. The sizeable community, then, needed a good courthouse to provide for the execution of civil law. As the first county seat, Duncan City had the honor of administering government for the fledging county, opening a courthouse there around 1853. But as Cheboygan grew, the county seat was relocated and so too the county's civil justice responsibilities. A modest courthouse was built on the corner of present-day Court and Huron Streets at a cost of $3,000. But by the middle of the 1890s, at the peak of Cheboygan's growth, it was evident that the existing structure was no longer an acceptable facility. When the previous courthouse had been built, the county population was 2,196; by the time the new one would be completed, it would be over fifteen thousand.[64]

By popular approval of the voters of Cheboygan County, in 1894 a new courthouse was authorized. After some debate about where the structure was to be built, it was agreed that the corner of Main and Court Streets, adjacent to the old courthouse, would be the best location. The Cheboygan Manufacturing Company then took over and diligently worked until the building was completed in 1898. The finishing touches were concluded early in 1900, at a final cost of about $35,000.[65] Despite the length of time necessary to finish the project and the fact that it was considerably over-budget, the Cheboygan County Courthouse became a stunning example of how an important building in an important city could demand a noteworthy presence. Complete with a large water fountain near the entrance, the courthouse and grounds were an inspiring testament to the hard working people of Cheboygan.

Each one of these businesses, buildings, and countless others all helped make Cheboygan what it was at the zenith of its development. While lumber made it all possible and employed more men than any other local industry, each business had its own part to play. Main Street was a cornucopia of trade and commerce and all sorts of people, from shanty boys and sawyers to doctors and lawyers. Saloons to libraries, Cheboygan had it all, a real hodgepodge of the evolving American nation.

A stroll downtown during this peak of prosperity and growth was a full workout for the senses. A constant aroma of cut wood and sawdust filled the air. Wood shavings and dust permeated everything and was scattered all over, trekked by the hundreds of mill employees as they made their way to and from work and to the sawdust-floored saloons. Whistles from steamboats entering and leaving the river alerted the residents of new arrivals of tourists, businessmen, or immigrants. The click-clack of horses hooves could be heard in between the conversations of tailors, photographers and barbers. A departing train chugs in the background as it bellows out smoke, struggling to pull its heavy load of new lumber. Strolling children do not notice this as they savor fresh, sweet candy from the Watermill Store, their laughter resonating over the bankers' and lawyers' discussions about politics. All the while steam rose from the mills and cast its shadow over Cheboygan, letting its residents know what was really in control – lumber.

5

Of Shanty Boys and Lumber Barons

The beginning of the twentieth century was a strange time for Cheboygan. It had enjoyed wealth, prosperity, a building boom, and economic security. Lumber had provided jobs and opportunities for the thousands of people who came there to work. Gradually, however, the predictions some had made decades earlier were beginning to become reality. While buildings were still being built and the community looked like it was still in the middle of a boom, it was literally running out of fuel. The problem with the lumber industry was that eventually the regional supply of raw material was going to be exhausted. The more mills there are in an area, the more quickly that supply dwindles. Faced with this reality, many of Cheboygan's mill operators closed up shop in the first part of the new century. Some moved west, while others such as W. & A. McArthur moved their operations north to Canada (who relocated to Little Current, Ontario in 1902).[1] Others tried to make the best of the situation in Cheboygan by floating logs from Canada (while it was still legal) or from the Upper Peninsula. Some also tried cutting other types of wood and adapting to the conditions as they were, turning what appeared to be a disadvantage into an advantage. Enter M.D. Olds.

There is perhaps no one man associated more with lumbering in Cheboygan than the enduring figure of Millard David Olds. By no means did he fit the mold of the typical lumber baron. He was very successful and wealthy, but it is there that the similarities ended. Unlike the predecessors of the W. & A. McArthur Company and so many other lumber firms, Olds did not get financing from anyone other than himself. He started his career humbly and through his dedication to hard

Millard David Olds (Image courtesy Olds family website).

work and fiscal conservativeness his life became a true "rags to riches" story. Crafty, resourceful, but yet a generous man, Olds forever left an indelible mark on the community which he was such a prominent part of. A man of varied interests, he owned a car ferry, railroads, and farm, had stakes in a sugar company in Ohio and a lumbering company in Oregon, and even made time to be a founding member of the Cheboygan Golf and Country Club. While other lumbermen would leave town after the boom had ended, Olds loved his cherished Cheboygan and would prefer to stay there rather than move on in order to make even more money. His legacy has created for himself a reputation which has far outlasted the lumber boom of which he played so pivotal a part.

Born on 10 March 1860 in Hartford, Michigan, M.D. Olds was the third of four children born to farmers Jerusha (née. Hurd) and Joseph

Ransom Olds. He was of very humble beginnings, working when he was a young man for two dollars a week in a stave mill. He entered the stave business for himself once he had saved up $400, moving north to Vanderbilt, Michigan and buying into a company owned by a Mr. Hixson.[2] While in partnership there, he learned a great deal about the business of buying timber and using it to manufacture broom handles, slack barrel elm and staves. He then moved to Cheboygan in 1892 and set up his own stave mill. Although this mill burned just a few years later in 1897, Olds promptly began his next venture by buying lands for lumber and dealing in timber as well. In 1904, Olds bought the Nelson & Clark mill near the mouth of the river's east side. At long last he had entered into the lumbering business for himself.[3] Olds gradually moved his way up the business ladder, starting ever so small and working his way up to becoming a member of that elite league of Cheboyganites who could call themselves "lumber barons." Meanwhile, this new player in the local market was plotting his next move.

The Nelson & Clark mill was a long-established business in Cheboygan. It was initially part of the Cheboygan Lumber Company, which had been founded in 1879. Around the turn of the century it was sold and became the Nelson & Clark mill, which at the time was one of the largest businesses in the city. Olds then bought the mill and changed the name to Olds Cheboygan Lumber Company, M.D. Olds & Company, and finally to M.D. Olds Lumber Company in 1904. As the harvesting of pine was beginning to wane around the turn of the century, it would appear on the surface that Olds made a foolish decision in purchasing the company. But fortunately for the would-be baron, demand was shifting away from pine and towards hardwoods, which left him in a most advantageous position.[4] Naturally this meant good things for Olds, but more importantly it meant good things for Cheboygan as well. Pine, however, was still the traditional staple of the region.[5]

Olds believed that he could do well in Cheboygan. His mills and docks produced and held a wide variety of wood products, as well as provided docking space for the many lake cruisers and tourist ships coming to the scenic north. By 1907, Olds' mill had a capacity of producing 100,000 feet of lumber every day and was running day and night. As mentioned previously, he had also purchased the McArthur docks located on the opposite side of the river, thus making his company the *de facto* controller of the mouth of the city's vitally important waterway. Both the old McArthur docks and Nelson & Clark docks jetted far out into Lake Huron, upon which could be stacked cut lumber (sometimes as high as twenty feet) waiting to be shipped to far away destinations. A series of breakwaters also were present to protect the elaborate system of dockage necessary to conduct as extensive an operation as Olds'.[6] Within the mill, Olds possessed some of the finest equipment in the industry, including a nine-foot and ten-foot Prescott band saw, two edgers, a trimmer, and a lathe mill; the mill itself was equipped with a 450-horespower Allis-Chalmers engine. There were four boilers, each measuring five by eighteen feet. According to Olds, "I think we have one of the best steaming plants and the best power of any mill I know of."[7] He possessed both access to the lumber and the means to produce it efficiently into a saleable product, which he wasted no time in doing.

The mill area on the east side of the river was quite intricate and vast, though not necessarily atypical of a large lumber processing facility of the day. The main building itself, which contained the saw mill and lath mill, was roughly 5200 square feet. Other items located on the site were a slab conveyor, twelve-foot high trestle, sorting platform, refuse burner, blacksmith's and carpenter's shops, and of course the hundreds of feet of dockage. A large log boom and piles of scattered slab wood covered a vast area to the south and east of the mill. In all, about 125 men were employed at any one time, not including those working out in the woods cutting and harvesting lumber before processing at the mill.[8]

Thankfully, a substantial amount is known about Olds and his operations. This knowledge provides a glimpse into how men lived and worked in the community at the time, what jobs people did, how operations in the mills were carried out, and what kinds of activities occurred on a daily basis. Consequently, it is now possible to learn more about the history of the community not just through numbers or facts and figures, but also by looking at the humanity of everyday life.

M.D. Olds & Company, about 1910 (Image © Johnson's Studio, all rights reserved).

Before the logging could begin, a lumber company such as Olds' first had to secure the rights to cut a tract of land or acquire wood. This could be done a number of ways. Options included outright purchase of land, purchase of standing timber, purchase of previously cut timber, or, before being banned by the Canadian government, the importation of foreign lumber for processing in the United States. Olds himself usually cut timber off his own land and then worked it in his mill. When he purchased the Nelson & Clark mill, included in the sale were the 40,000 acres that the company owned, and so they passed into Olds' substantial holdings.[9] In the early days of logging, property could be secured through a United States Land office such as that which was located in Duncan City. This land was usually sold in large parcels for the giveaway price of $1.25 an acre (with the requirement that it be purchased in parcels of eighty [later forty] acres or more, thus preventing the average person from jumping in on this deal). However, once all the property had been bought up, it had to be bought from whoever the current owner(s) was.

The actual process of lumbering was always initiated by a man known as the timber estimator or cruiser. It was his duty to visit a tract of land to determine what each section held in terms of marketable timber. The detailed reports these men created divided up a small section of land and gave an analysis of what was in each. For example, in the northwest corner of the northwest corner of township thirty-seven north, range one east, section 8, estimator John Lyberg indicated on 16 November 1906 that there were forty hemlock trees, five maple, five beech, two birch, and that the locale was "part plains." Other descriptions in nearby areas indicated that the land was "½ cut and plains," "bushy," or that "5 ac. [acres] in SE corner bad."[10] This was unquestionably tedious work, but nevertheless was absolutely necessary to determine what tracts of land were worth harvesting and in what order. Accurate timber estimates were required to plan out a season's logging, and if not done properly, could cause the lumberman economic ruin. The lumbering operations had to be planned out well or a profit would not be made – and if there was one thing all of the lumber barons was interested in, it was making as much money as possible.

Once the land had been purchased and surveyed and the best place to log had been determined, the lumbermen moved in. Only the most physically fit and strong men needed apply for these jobs, as the workday was long and very demanding. Lumber camps were built at a strategically located site, and generally had four or five buildings, depending on the size of the operation. This included two or three bunkhouses for the men, a cook house, and a company store. The actual cutting of the timber (or "felling") was only one part of the job. Initially, trees would be cut down by skilled fellers using a double-headed ax, usually with two men per tree. Later the ax fell into disuse as it was replaced by the two-man crosscut saw, which was faster and easier to use. Once the fellers had done their job, swampers would then trim any limbs from the tree and cut away the bark on one side to facilitate stacking. Depending on the size, final destination, and mode of transportation of the wood, it could then be cut (or "bucked") into smaller, more manageable logs.[11]

It should be noted that each lumber camp, depending on its geographical location, could have a variety of different jobs which needed to be carried out. A typical camp would include a foreman and store clerk, teamsters, sawyers, swampers (for cutting the recently fallen logs), a blacksmith, filer (for keeping saws sharp), cook, cook's assistant (cookie), and choreboy.[12] Other men would be responsible for skidding, bunching, hauling, loading, and cutting. Generally men did the same thing from season to season, although it could vary depending on the types of jobs needed to be done and what time of year logging was conducted in.

It was not an easy life. Lawrence Boucha, a cookie at several northern Michigan lumber camps, including one belonging to Embury-Martin, knew the life of the lumbermen first hand. "You got up at four o'clock in the mornin' and you never saw the bed till long after dark," he described. Laboring from sunup to sundown was the norm, and work was done six days per week. At the end of the day the men would return to their bunkhouse, where their wet clothes would be hung to dry. Ice would form from the nails sticking through the tarpaper roof, and the smell of body odor, sweat and grime was atrocious.[13]

Bathing was as rare as cleaning clothes. Boucha joked, perhaps not so untruthfully, that the men's clothes would move on their own after awhile because of the rampant infestation of unwelcome critters. By the end of a season it is no wonder, then, that the men headed back into town to find a barber where they could rent a bath and clean up. Most men would be back next year for another season, but some found the life too taxing and never returned.[14]

There was another job which was essential to the logging operation, especially in the days before the railroads. Swampers had the job of cutting out a road known as a tote road, which was the path out of the forest to a body of water or a predetermined stacking and sorting area for the logs. In the winter, this ideally straight and level road would be sprinkled with water to allow it to freeze and so make the transportation of large quantities of timber on sleds that much easier. Skidders would take sections of the recently felled timber and move them to the decking

A typical Cheboygan County lumber camp scene, about 1890 (Image © Johnson's Studio, all rights reserved).

grounds (piling areas) along the tote road.[15] Logs would then be loaded on logging sleighs, often stacked far beyond their safe capacity, and hauled along the road. Another job, far less glorious than the romantic images of loggers hacking down giant pine trees, was that of the road monkey. This individual was responsible for the less-dramatic job of removing piles of horse feces which had fallen along the tote road. The purpose of this profession was not cosmetic. Logging sleds, once they were in motion, could be very hard to stop. Essentially, they were giant toboggans stacked with wood and sliding on ice; if anything got in the way of these sleighs carrying thousands of pounds of weight, the result could be disastrous for any teamster driving it or anyone else who happened to be standing too close to the mass of moving timber. Any foreign objects along the path of these sleighs had to be removed, especially before something like a big pile of excrement froze up solid.

The road monkey did not have a particularly exciting job, but the lives of the teamster and any others alongside the sleigh were counting on him. As if the piles of defecate were not enough, the dangerous, steep downward grade of the tote road could pose another set of problems. To combat this, sand was thrown on the ice to impede a would-be runaway sleigh from going down the road like a sled on ice.[16]

Once the logs had been hauled to their proper place, the cut timber would be stacked at rollways along bodies of frozen water or the decking grounds near a railroad, both via the tote road. When the springtime thaws came the drive could begin. Logs were rolled into the river and floated (the "drive") to a mill location, such as those in Cheboygan and Duncan City. Jams in the river ("dead heads") posed a constant problem. If the body of logs inching its way down the river got caught, any further movement would be impossible. Men known as river drivers had the exceedingly dangerous task of walking on top of the floating mass as it floated down river, loosening jams and pulling stray logs back into the fold. His only equipment for this task was an eight to twelve foot long pike pole, cant hook, peavey and spiked shoes.[17] If the driver lost his balance, the result could easily be an untimely demise under the river of wood.

Each of the thousands and thousands of logs floating down to the mills had to be marked with a logmark to identify the owner. In the late nineteenth century there were dozens of different lumber barons in the area and equally many marks, with some companies having multiple. M.D. Olds alone had several, including "MD & Co," a sideways M inside a D, and one with the letters HJ. Although it is not absolutely certain what this latter logmark stood for, it is most likely in honor of his mother, Jerusha Herd.[18]

As this lumber floated downstream it often plugged the rivers and made them impossible to navigate, creating the most inconvenient problem of the log jam, or dead head. As previously discussed, a boom company was eventually organized to help sort out the floating lumber, the Cheboygan Slack Water Navigation Company, in 1867.[19] Nevertheless, it could still take several days for just one drive of a company's logs to pass through. In April 1903 lumberman Sam Gilpin's logs took three days to sort, which consisted of an estimated 1.5 million feet of lumber.[20] Despite this seasonal congestion of the river, however, there was usually no lack of productivity for Cheboygan's lumber mills.

Fortunately for any would-be river captains, around the turn of the century it became increasingly common to use railroads to move timber rather than the rivers. Not only did this clear up some congestion, it also made it possible to transport lumber year-round. M.D. Olds operated three small railroads himself for this purpose.[21] Other railroads ran into mills such as W. & A. McArthur and Embury-Martin, as well as into the Pfister & Vogel Leather Company, all of which were spurs off the Michigan Central.[22]

In the case of Embury-Martin, an additional special locomotive was in use. Dubbed the "Hemlock Special," it was built to run not on standard steel rails, but on self-propelled caterpillar treads to crawl on the snow. Manufactured in Lima, Ohio and Eau Claire, Wisconsin, there were two of these machines in operation in Cheboygan. One was owned by M.D. Olds; the other, utilized by Embury-Martin, was owned by George Michelin. Both these devices could trek right on the compacted snow much like how an army tank rumbles along the field of battle, a testament to the innovative lumber barons and their employees.[23]

Back in the camps, it was not uncommon for men to remain there for extended periods of time, doing little but working, sleeping, and eating. Rarely leaving the camp, men would buy from the camp store any supplies they needed. Items purchased would be placed on an individual's personal account, and before being paid at the end of the season, the amount owed would be deduced from their wages. Common things such as shoe laces, suspenders, underwear, socks, pants, and gloves were all required in order to work and get the job done. But remembering the humanity of all these workers as well, the tough lumbermen also bought envelopes and stamps to write to family, friends and loved ones about their daily life in a northern Michigan lumber camp.[24]

That life was by no means an easy one. Accidents were exceedingly frequent, and the health of anyone working out in the woods was not something he would take for granted.

Lumbering was a hazardous business and injuries and accidental deaths were very common. Men were injured by falling branches, pinned and crushed by trees that fell contrary to expectation, and crippling or fatal gashes on feet, legs, arms, or head resulted from saws and axes. Loading and hauling of the logs caused many accidents. Broken arms or legs and crushed bodies resulted from the breaking of sleighs or failure of equipment... Contagious disease sometimes ravaged the men from the camps... Camp operators usually felt no financial responsibility to the men so injured, but some few did aid their injured employees. More often a collection was taken up among the fellow workmen.[25]

One of these collections occurred shortly after the death of a man by the name of Lewis Wright, who was killed while working for M.D. Olds on 22 July 1910. Most of the men were quite generous in their contributions, with donated amounts ranging anywhere from twenty-five cents to five dollars.[26] In addition to the expected types of injuries resulting from handling large and bulky objects like logs, there were other concerns to be wary of as well. Drinking water at the camp well was not necessarily of the greatest purity, and there is at least one reported case of typhoid fever that was caused by a contaminated well.[27] Although this case is atypical, physically crippling injuries were not. Everyday there was a chance a man could be gashed, maimed, or killed. The frequency with which this occurred undoubtedly left imprinted in each worker a sense of his own mortality. It is no surprise, then, that after the men were paid at the end of the season and made their way into town, they enjoyed "living it up" at the saloons and with ladies of the night.

The men who worked in the camps were a special breed. Due to the tough living conditions and unrelenting hard labor, it was a place where one could expect to be tested to the maximum of his physical abilities. The lumber camp truly was a place where one could become "a man among men." But this is not to say that they were an impersonal lot of rough and tough guys. Rather, they were instead "cordial, good-natured, free hearted fellows, capable of appreciating a good joke and fully competent to return the same." An excerpt from *The Manitawauba Chronicle* around the time the first lumber camps in the area were being established provides a glimpse into the daily life.

> In the middle camp, where there are thirty-five men all told, about 50,000 ft. are put into the river per day. There are four men, two choppers and two sawyers-who average 100 pieces per day and I held the watch while two men went through a log 26 inches in diameter in just 1 ¾ minutes.[28]

In order to be able to work at this rate, the men had to be well fed. Camp cooks were usually held in high esteem for their ability to cook good bread, biscuits, beans, pies and gingerbread. Men in the camps always had plenty to eat and the food was nutritious and satisfying. Talking was usually not permitted at the table, excepting the polite request to pass the rolls. As soon as a man had eaten his dinner, he had to promptly excuse himself. Conversation could lead to a heated argument, and the dinner table at a lumber camp with dozens of rowdy men was not the best place for that. Considering the demanding nature of the work, each meal was a welcome break from the strenuous labor of taming the northern wilderness.

Life in the lumber camps was, of course, focused on work. Sunday was the only day off, and it was a welcome opportunity to make conversation, relax, clean up, play games or just give the body a chance to rest. Generally there was no alcohol allowed at any time in the camp. Imbibing would be an obvious detriment to getting much done the following morning, and so the no-booze rule was strictly enforced. When the shanty boys came back into town, though, one of the first places many of them headed to was their favorite watering hole.

Although it is perhaps a bit romantic to think about the rugged frontier men coming in from the camps to celebrate the end of a season back in town by enjoying the night life and frequenting any of the innumerable saloons, this simply did not happen in the typically fancied way. While yes, many of the single men working in the camps were footloose and fancy free once they got back from weeks or months of being cooped up in the woods with no real entertainment, most of them were only employed in the work seasonally and after the lumber had been cut, they went back to their farms and resumed work there. Before the days when locomotives made transporting logs possible at any time of the year, most loggers were only seasonal employees. They farmed during the late spring and summer, and as the harvest came in and the weather got cooler and snow began to fall, it was time to head out into the woods to cut trees. This worked out well because these men then had year-round employment, farming half the year and lumbering the rest. While this was not how every shanty boy eked out his existence, it was very common for the men of the Cheboygan area.

Once all the felling, cutting, and other jobs had been finished and the lumber had finally made its way to the mill, it was time to begin the work of making the finished product. At M.D. Olds' mill at the peak of its production, the work was nearly constant and around the clock. On a typical day, the mills started cutting at 6:45 A.M. They would then stop at noon for a forty-five minute lunch break. Another break at 6:00 P.M. for a shift change, and then back to work until midnight. Another forty-five minute break then followed, and then cutting continued until 3:00 A.M. A half-hour rest was then afforded, and the mill started back up and cut until 6:00. At 6:45, the next day's shifts started. Saturday was a full day of work (until 1:30 Sunday morning), but Sundays were a day off, saving a single watchman.[29] At 6:45 Monday morning it was back to work cutting up more northern Michigan lumber. Equipment problems could hold up the daily production at any time, and such tribulations were annoyingly frequent.

Even though the actual lumbering and driving of logs to the mills may have been the most dangerous part, work in the mills was not much safer. The logs to be cut were large and cumbersome, not to mention the fact that the work itself involved large saws and heavy equipment. In the mill itself, injuries such as smashed fingers and toes, broken ribs, dislocated shoulders, head cuts, and serious bruises were all common. In the most severe cases, amputation was sometimes necessary. Other opportunities for great bodily injury could result from mechanical failures. "J.B. McArthur met with a bad breakdown at his saw mill, Friday of last week, the large fly wheel bursting into several pieces, cutting the driving belt in two, one piece flying to the end of the mill, striking a six inch square Norway pine brace, and cutting through it like a knife."[30] Incidents like these were not rare and all but added to the dangerous work faced by those employed in the industry.

Working outside the mill did not mean one was any less susceptible to danger. Falling pieces of lumber while loading or just plain tripping on crowded docks caused many injuries. In a more dramatic example, on 18 April 1911, a man in the employ of Olds named Walter P. Fike, aged fifty-five, fell to his death as he was about to put a screen on the smokestack at the Olds mill. As he fell he hit the base of the smokestack and fell into the water. He was immediately fished out by coworkers but died three hours later.[31]

While this is a case which is out of the ordinary, daily injuries either in the woods or at the mill were common. Rightly or wrongly, blame was often placed on the injured person, who could expect little in the way of compensation. Sometimes, however, the injured person did receive pay comparable to what they would have made in the time they missed while recovering from their injuries.[32] Anyone employed in the harvesting and processing of logs was at risk for substantial injuries at any time, with very few exceptions. The work was exceedingly labor intensive, physically demanding, and always dangerous.

As the logs had been cut and processed in the mills, it was essential to keep accurate and detailed records of how much timber was manufactured. Like other lumbermen, Olds kept comprehensive daily reports of the amount of lumber that he cut. In one typical week in June, 1908, daily production ranged between 60,630 and 73,725 feet, with an average per day of 68,474, and a total for the week of 410,845 feet. Later in the year production was slightly higher, with large quantities of hemlock making up a majority of that which was cut, with lesser quantities of white pine, Norway spruce, tamarack, basswood, ash, elm and birch, among others. From this harvested wood would eventually come lumber, lath, staves and pickets.[33] After all the wood was cut, it was moved onto the docks, neatly stacked, and made ready for shipping.

One of the perpetual problems inherent with such a large quantity of wood is the fact that it was easily combustible. Far too often both lumber and mills were damaged or destroyed by fire. On 28 October

1911, Olds himself fell victim to this persistent problem. A fire broke out on one of the breakwater docks, causing a significant amount of white pine and maple to be burned or lost. A fire on a lumber dock was more than just a fire, however. Lumber that was in danger of catching fire had to be thrown into the water, sometimes recovered and sometimes not. Workers had to be paid for throwing the lumber in, fishing it out after the fire, and for restacking it. Even a tugboat owner had to be paid for his assistance in fighting the blaze. Although Olds had $33,000 in combined coverage (from twelve different insurance companies) in case of just such an even as this, the claim was only for $466.80, of which he was paid the full amount.[34]

Fires such as this were by no means infrequent. Less common were fires of greater magnitude, such as that which ravished much of northern Michigan in October 1908. This blaze incinerated thousands of acres, dozens of homes and businesses, and completely destroyed the village of Metz in nearby Presque Isle County. Although the fire spared Cheboygan, a great deal of timber to the east of town was destroyed in the inferno. Olds owned just over 16,000 acres of timber in this region, not including other standing timber he had which was destroyed. In all, he lost between twenty and twenty-one thousand acres.[35]

The loss of such a great deal of timber was a direct contribution to the eventual closing of the Olds mill in 1916. Olds was counting on being able to use the wood on this land until about 1920 or 1923, but after the fire he believed that he would only be able to do so until around 1914 or 1915. In a letter to his daughter, he explained his dejection. "This timber was what I was saving to cut seven or eight years from now when I could not get enough logs to keep the mill running from other places... but now we have got to lumber that first and won't be able to get logs more than six or seven years."[36] Olds' plans for the next several years had hit a snag.

The reason this lumber had to be cut first was attributable to the nature of the fire which burned it. As the flames spread across the region, it burned mostly the tops of trees and scorched the bark, rather than completely burning the wood. This does not completely destroy the tree, but rather kills the bark and causes the tree to die slowly. What is more, because the majority of the standing timber in this land was hemlock, the damaged bark had to be peeled almost immediately so that it could be used to make hemlock extract at the Tannery before it rotted.[37]

The losses that Olds suffered as a result of the October 1908 fire are truly staggering. He estimated that he had lost some $300,000 as the market currently stood, but had the timber been cut under better conditions, the loss would have approached something closer to half a million dollars. On the bark alone he lost over $100,000, and the white pine that was lost amounted to $75,000. It is very difficult to absorb a loss of this magnitude, even for a man like Olds. Complicating the matter was the necessity of building a railroad into his burned acreage so that the wood could be carried out. Because Olds was not planning to cut this timber for several years there was no railroad yet in place.[38] The road he eventually built, about eighteen miles long, had two locomotives to haul the cars carrying logs that were cut directly to his mill. At night, his employees slept in cars on the tracks.[39]

Years after the fire Olds was still suffering its effects. In the spring of 1910, some of his employees had gone out to survey the unfortunate situation. What they saw was not encouraging. "…The trees had all blown down one on top of the other until they were nine deep where they stood. When they got up on top so they could look around, they could see just four trees standing." While the fire did not render such complete destruction on all his land, it sadly meant that much of what he was counting on for future production was lost. Of the 16,000 acres which were damaged or destroyed from the fire, Olds indicated in October 1911 that there would be a sizeable quantity he would never bother with. "Out of the sixteen thousand acres we had east of here I think there will be five to six thousand acres that we will not touch at all… it is in such a condition and so much of it poor that it is not worth getting out. Therefore, we never will touch it." Much of the wood had by this time died, fallen down, or begun to rot. This makes handling and cutting the wood much more expensive, as the timber is both rough and dirty, and this easily dulls the saws. What made the matter worse was the fact that for the lumber which was saved, much of it could not be peeled.[40] In this unfortunate situation the decay of Olds' lumbering enterprise had begun.

There was a bit of a silver lining to the fire. Part of the burned region, known as the "High Banks," consisted of virgin hemlock and was owned by the Pfister & Vogel Leather Company. When the fire came through, the firm's trees were burned and bark scorched. Olds capitalized on the situation by purchasing stumpage rights to the damaged (but not destroyed) standing timber. He then cut the trees, sawed them into lumber, and sold the bark to the Tannery. As another accidental benefit of the fire, other lumber companies from neighboring communities such as Alpena, Millersburg, and Onaway were provided with thousands of acres now available for winter logging operations, as the timber had to be cut down immediately.[41] But in the end, the fire caused more damage than a mere glancing of the statistics would indicate. The long-term effects on the local economy, such as those suffered by Olds, far outweighed the few positive effects. With several years' lumber cut ruined, future growth and productivity was greatly handicapped.

Another problem that occurred less frequently but still was a potential trouble was the risk of inadvertently purchasing illegally harvested lumber – that is, lumber cut from federal lands. In one case, the United States government alleged that Olds had purchased wood from George and William McDonald, valued at $146.25. This wood had purportedly been cut during the winter of 1904-1905, although this allegation did not come about until 1909. Undoubtedly he could have paid the amount he supposedly owed, but he was not about to concede so easily. His prompt response to the United States was both gentlemanly and firm. "Now as I told you before, if I got the logs and am holden for them, it is not necessary to sue me, but as I did not buy the logs from these gentlemen, if these gentlemen stole the government's timber, it seems to me this is a very poor way to catch the thief – make somebody else pay and let the thief go. But possibly that is the best way."[42] While it is unknown whether or not Olds paid the amount, it is clear who he thought was right. (The amount the government claimed here was exceedingly small, even by the standards of the day. In another similar case from the same time, Olds owed the Department of the Interior $280, which amounted to 40,000 feet of pine, spruce, balsam and tamarack. On a typical production day, this would represent less than half of a day's work. It is unlikely Olds would even have remembered such a transaction if it occurred at all, being now four years prior, and that is assuming he personally carried out the transaction, which is highly improbable).

Conflagrations and federal intimidation notwithstanding, the actual selling of the finished lumber, lath, staves, and pickets now became the objective. M.D. Olds & Co. was not a retail lumber store open to the general public. Rather, Olds sold to other large companies who would bring their ships to his docks, load up, and be on their way. This process began by a particular buyer expressing desire to purchase a certain sizeable quantity of lumber. A contract or memorandum of sale would then be drawn up and sent to the buyer. As soon as the contract was signed, the agreement was binding. The memorandums of sale described the type, thickness, price and amount of lumber the purchaser was agreeing to buy, as well as by when it was to be removed from the seller's docks. These purchasers were often a considerable distance away, typically near the lower Great Lakes, and so a third-party inspector of the wood would be necessary to insure that everyone was being fair. There were a goodly amount of inspectors in the Cheboygan area, including W.L. Martin, E.H. Silliman, and William P. DeKlyne, among others. Assuming the lumber was acceptable it was loaded onto the buyer's ships and carried away. The Saginaw Bay Company of Cleveland, J.M. Hastings Company of Sandusky, Ohio and Estabrook-Skeele Lumber Company of Chicago are but a few of those companies which did business with Olds.[43] There were literally dozens of others.

Not all of the companies that Olds did business with were far away. The Pfister & Vogel Leather Company liked doing business with Olds, and luckily for him, the company was constantly in need of bark for use in the production of its finished leather. Olds was in a position to supply a good amount of this bark to the Tannery. By 1 April 1910, for example, he was to deliver 2200 pounds of bark priced for $9.75, with some eight to twenty thousand cords to follow later that year and into 1911.[44] In this way, he was able to make an honest buck from a product that there otherwise would have been little demand for. Olds was a meticulous and astute lumber baron through and through, and made a dime any way he could.

Olds, "perhaps one of the shrewdest lumbermen that ever lived in Cheboygan,"[45] was always looking for a way to make a profit, and was often quite crafty when it came to doing so. To cite but one example, ships often used waste products from the mills such as sawdust and small pieces of wood as fuel – but with the increased use of coal, this potential source of revenue was literally going up in smoke as it was now unneeded and tossed into the refuse burner. Some other sort of use had to be devised for this waste product. Around 1910, the ever-thrifty Olds turned to the production of wood chips (made from excess slabs, edgings and "fine stuff") to fire the burners for the Cheboygan Paper Company (formerly the W. & A. McArthur Lumber Company), which required 125 tons of chips every twenty-four hours.[46] The wood that had heretofore been used in fueling ships and homes (but with not nearly enough demand) was now being used to fuel the production of paper. Olds indicated that within one nine-month period, $15,129 worth of chips was sold to the paper mill, of which sixty percent was profit. He pointed out that while this sounds like a substantial amount of money, some places were able to take all of their excess wood material and use it for making other products such as charcoal and wood alcohol. Olds himself did not have the means to do this, and so was able to only use a part of the wood.[47]

Playing the changing Michigan lumber market was a skill that Olds had a particular affinity for. Had he not been so crafty, it is unlikely he would have done any better than all of the other mill operators in Cheboygan who were forced to leave at the turn of the century, due primarily to the exhaustion of white pine supplies. Fortunately, other types of lumber were also in high demand, including hemlock, birch, and maple, the latter becoming increasingly common for use in flooring.

Olds cut whatever he could, but far and away the most lumber that he cut was hemlock. In October 1908, nearly forty-four percent of all the wood he had on his docks was hemlock, even though some ten other kinds were on hand as well.[48] Steadily rising prices of this wood helped contribute to Olds' increasing wealth. While other woods were more valuable than white pine (double in some cases), the sheer volume of hemlock that Olds sold made up the price gap. White pine, although still harvested, was not present in sufficient quantity as it once was to generate wealth for myriad lumbermen. Regardless, Olds was still able to make his fortune and live the prosperous life in Cheboygan that he did, even in a time when others were mourning the decline of the predominant local industry.

Olds' success was by any standard exemplary, especially considering the period in which he made his fortune and his lack of good luck. When other lumber barons and would-be fortune seekers were looking to the west and to Canada for other timber lands to cut, Olds stayed in Cheboygan, craftily applying his knowledge of the market and the region to garner significant economic gains. But even his intrepid entrepreneurial spirit would not be enough to guard Cheboygan from the shifting winds of change which were beginning to blow across the Straits. The 1920s would usher in a new era for Cheboygan, one in which the lumber boom and the subsequent prosperity the city enjoyed were becoming part of a gilded memory. With the depletion of lumber, Cheboygan was forced to cope with the reality that she was not going to be as prosperous as she was just a decade or two previously. Moreover, a series of unfortunate events greatly exacerbated what was already a difficult situation.

6

Winds of Change

An inevitable part of any boom town is that eventually the boom loses its thunder. They spring up in a hurry, and if there is nothing to sustain them after their fuel is exhausted, they turn into forgotten settlements and antiquated relics. While Cheboygan did find greater purpose after its lumber supply, and source of prosperity, had been expended, it was not immediately clear that this was going to be the case. Everyone wanted to believe that there would be a good future in Cheboygan, but this was a hard idea to sell on those who were gradually losing their jobs and whose families were going hungry. Cheboygan's economy was in a period of great instability and fluctuation as the community struggled to find its economic niche.

Despite the success of lumber barons like Olds, the same could not be said for the city as a whole. The antithesis of the prosperous lumber days was now the predominant problem of white pine exhaustion and resident depopulation. With less lumber, manufacturing businesses had no reason to stay in Cheboygan, and doing so would only have spelled ruin for most of them if they had. The inevitable result was a rapid loss of jobs and people. Between 1889 and 1929 the average number of employees in the county among those establishments declined a staggering eighty-two percent.[1] Not only is declination such as this difficult economically, but socially as well. For those that do decide to stay in town, the pressure for good jobs and adequate social interaction with like-minded people presents a formidable challenge.

As early as 1907 the Cheboygan Chamber of Commerce began promoting Cheboygan as a tourist and resort area. It would take some twenty years, however, before there was any notable recovery for the tremendously hard hit city.[2] From a very early day, Cheboygan was a popular destination for tourists, and this fact should not be glossed over. However, its primary function and purpose as a city was as a lumbering and industrial area, not a nice place to come and relax for a week, although certainly many did. The difference now was that Cheboygan would have to rely on tourism, rather than enjoy its fruits as a beneficial side effect of the lumber boom.

By 1916, the lumber industry was on its last legs, even for the resourceful M.D. Olds. After a long and very profitable run as a prolific lumber baron in Cheboygan, it was time to close the mill and seek other business ventures. In August of that year, he wrote to the Bartlett Lumber Company of Shelldrake, Michigan, that "there isn't enough timber around here to stock the mill in full, therefore I have decided not to operate...."[3] Instead of running twenty-four hours a day, six days per week, Olds was now operating his mill during the day and only seasonally at that.[4] Although not the last mill to operate in Cheboygan, the closing of the Olds mill was a great detriment to not only the workers it employed, but also to the community as well. Such a move could not be called unexpected by any means, and probably was already much delayed. While Olds did go on to sell coal and continue to have ships use his docks, his lumbering interests in the community were over.

With the decreasing number of seasonal workers passing through Cheboygan it is to be expected that the overall makeup of the city would change in kind. For some, during this time a greater sense of permanency began to take form. Places such as the Opera House were in operation for live entertainment, and the Kingston Theatre was available for both live shows and the new novelty of motion pictures. Both became fashionable places to associate. The presence of establishments such as these show that people had some leisure time and enjoyed doing things for their own sake, rather than constantly working in the mills or delivering coal. Cheboygan was no longer a boom town, *per se*, but was becoming a permanent settlement which would live on long after all the timber was cut down and sold. For those that chose to stay, the question now became one of finding adequate employment.

View from the W. & A. McArthur Docks after being purchased by
M.D. Olds. Olds' mill is in the background (Image © Johnson's Studio,
all rights reserved).

Nineteen twenty-two was a particularly tough year for Cheboygan.
In March a fire erupted in the downtown which caused damage and
destruction the likes of which the city had not seen before or since. With
extensive property damage and loss of life, it was an event which,
although painfully destructive and violent, solidified the community in a
way in which prior to this it had never been.

Early in the morning on Wednesday, 8 March 1922, a carelessly
discarded cigarette ignited a pile of papers in the basement of the Frost-
Kessler building in the heart of Cheboygan's business district. The
janitor of the nearby First National Bank saw smoke rising from the top
of the building. He immediately called the telephone switchboard
operator, and the fire department was dispatched and soon arrived on

Cheboygan River looking north, 1910. This image also depicts the last log drive in the river.

the scene. Northern Michigan winters, long known for their length and deep frigidity, made firefighting exceedingly difficult. The three closest fire hydrants were frozen solid and could not be used; consequently the fire continued to spread. Being in such close proximity to the Frost-Kessler building, the First National Bank quickly caught fire as the flames jumped across Division Street. The city landmark was ignited somewhere near the top, and then hellstorm made its way down. The metal roofing held the fire in, preventing any water from being applied to the raging inferno. The fire spread from business to business, but was finally held in check by a fire wall when it reached the Post Hardware Company to the north of the bank.[5]

Back on the south side of Division Street, the fire began to consume the White House Bakery. Its proprietor, Frank Hohler, was trying to save as much as he could inside the building. Not having any insurance on his bakery or equipment, he ran in and out gathering whatever he could, attempting to haul it away to keep it protected from the carnage. Two teenage boys, George Tobias and Edward J. Laway, Jr., were assisting Hohler as the building next door began to collapse. A small part of the nearby wall of the Frost-Kessler block collapsed onto the roof of Hohler's building, and the cascading mass of flames, brick and ash rained down upon the men. Hohler screamed once or twice but then he, Tobias and Laway soon expired, their lives cut short by the awful tragedy.[6]

By around ten o'clock in the morning the fire was contained. The success of the firefighters' noble deeds was greatly attributable to the lack of winds. Nevertheless, the fire damage was extensive. Property loss was estimated between $250,000 and $500,000, and many businesses, offices, and fraternal organizations lost not only their meeting place but their records as well. Four business blocks (Hohler's Bakery, Frost-Kessler, First National Bank and Gerow Buildings) had all been completely destroyed or heavily damaged.

Despite the destruction done to the city, everyone pulled together and helped in any way they could. Fire equipment was sent on train to Cheboygan from Wolverine and Vanderbilt. At the paper company, the mill pumps injected water directly into the city mains, thus making sure that there was a constant supply of water going into the city to fight the fire. Mr. Lawler of the Pfister & Vogel Tannery sent as many hoses as he could (how many is unknown), as well as the men to operate them. Lastly, many volunteers helped fight the blaze. To the credit of the rest of the community, bystanders were for the most part orderly and did not cause any harmful interference with the firefighting efforts.[7]

Although so much had been lost, the one thing that clearly remained was hope. As the *Cheboygan Democrat* opined:

> Cheboygan has lost four very fine business blocks, each one a credit to the city and institutions we can ill afford to lose, as they housed some of the most important and prominent institutions of our city... Undoubtedly better and more modern places of business will grow up on the places now laying [sic] charred and burned and the scar will be effaced almost before we have recovered from telling about the city's biggest fire.

There was even a bit of humor to be found:

> W.L. Barr, on looking at the *Democrat* office [located behind the bank] standing unscathed ventured the remark, "That the devil looked after his own." That is not very complimentary, but then knowing Mr. Barr as we do, we can see that he meant to spring a joke on us in the midst of the holocust [sic], by utilizing the old saw.[8]

The fire was devastating, but new businesses did indeed promptly rise after the destruction. Though the bank was completely destroyed, the vault did its job well and thoroughly protected its valuable contents. The bank was able to reopen for business very quickly, with offices set up in the Milliken Garage across the street as early as the following day, despite the fact that they were "a little crowded." Other businesses, however, were not so lucky. The Michigan State Telephone Company suffered great losses, as did the Woolworth Five and Ten Store. Doctors, lawyers, grocers and an art and novelty dealer lost most everything they had, including equipment, records and merchandise. The majority of these individuals carried at least partial insurance, although some did not, which jeopardized any hope they had of reopening once everything had settled down and life returned to a sense of normality.[9]

Despite the severity of the fire's damage to much of the downtown, thanks can be given that none of the city's major industries burned that day. Although the fire spread quickly among downtown's closely-built structures, the industrial facilities were all well out of harm's way and so did not catch fire. Had they done so, a great many men would have been out of work, and there was no guarantee that these businesses would have been rebuilt, seriously weakening the economic base of a community that was already dealing with the decline of the lumber industry. For those that stayed after the lumbering heyday, jobs were not nearly as plentiful as they were before. But because Cheboygan was still an important city (although arguably less now that less lumber was being produced there), the downtown was quickly rebuilt and life returned to much like it was prior to the blaze. Sadly, the splendor and size of the buildings which replaced the old structures were not comparable, and four aesthetically pleasing, architecturally significant buildings were lost forever. A great deal of Cheboygan's early history burned on that tragic day. Nevertheless, like the phoenix the people of Cheboygan rose from the ashes and carried on, taking the catastrophe in stride and continuing on.

Just a few years later, another major business was stricken with hardship. Although not physically destructive, the economic destruction caused by the closing of the Tannery meant the exhaustion of jobs and livelihoods. After booming success in the leather industry during the First World War, postwar depression brought significant losses to Pfister & Vogel's Cheboygan Tannery. As the 1920s began the situation improved little; government regulations, tariff changes, litigation, international turmoil and importation of cheap European leathers all caused significant problems for the industry as a whole.[10] Local problems compounded the situation. The supply of hemlock bark, so essential to the tanning process, was gradually being exhausted. Therefore, in 1926 the Cheboygan Tannery closed its doors. The following year the property was sold to a wrecking crew and the buildings dismantled.[11] The massive buildings on the south end of town, so long a fixture of Cheboygan itself, were quickly removed. Thus, the city within a city was gone, and with it plenty of good, steady jobs.

Even with the devastation which plagued Cheboygan at the beginning of the 1920s, there were encouraging signs for the future as well. As manufacturing became less prolific, tourism gradually became more important. More and more people began making their way to Cheboygan to visit and enjoy the area. The number of visitors to state parks in Cheboygan County went up significantly throughout the twenties. In 1923 the total attendance for Aloha State Park was 5,553; by 1928, the attendance was 8,735, an increase of nearly sixty-five percent. Cheboygan State Park also showed rapid growth, with over three thousand more patrons visiting the park in 1928 than in the previous year. The reasons for this growth are likely varied; however, one key component is unquestionably greater accessibility to the automobile. With people free to travel and get away from the hustle and bustle of life even just for a weekend, Cheboygan's natural beauty and access to lakes and rivers provided innumerable places to experience solitude and refuge. As Dr. Gerow said some fifty years prior, if one is "in search of some locality where he may recuperate his vital powers, and after remaining here for even a short time, he goes back to his business with renewed zest and vigor," Cheboygan was the place to be.[12]

The lumbering industry held on in Cheboygan as long as it could. The death knells could be heard ringing from far off, but it was not until 1928 that the final chapter, so to speak, was written. It was in that year that the last significant lumber mill, the Embury-Martin Lumber Co., burned to the ground.

Operated by Harris Embury and William Martin, in 1907 this facility had a capacity of cutting 100,000 feet every 10 hours. It operated day and night and was complete with a saw mill, shingle mill, a refuse burner, machine shop, blacksmith shop, five docks, and various other buildings.[13]

On 15 November 1928, at around 11:30 A.M., a fire broke out at the Embury-Martin mill. A spark from an incinerator where chips were being burned quickly spread into a fire, which within forty-five minutes destroyed the facility. Early hopes that the fire alarms were nothing but routine drills were quickly extinguished when the city alarm was sounded. A flood of curious onlookers made their way out to see the big mill aflame like dry kindling. The efforts of the fire department and the mill employees were exceptionally brave and heroic, but even the eleven streams of water and countless volunteers battling the fire did not succeed quickly enough to save the mill.[14]

The fire which destroyed the Embury-Martin Lumber Company was compounded "by one of the strongest winds that ever swept Northern

The Embury-Martin Lumber Company, about 1907 (Image © Johnson's Studio, all rights reserved).

Michigan," and thus the destruction was both thorough and rapid. This type of event was not all that unusual, however. Prior to this most recent fire, the mill had burned three times, and each time the mill was rebuilt immediately after. Despite the fact that 1928 had seen a good cut of wood for the mill, it would not mean that the owners would be willing to reopen a fourth time. Even though the owners "were pleased with the future business outlook" in the area, apparently they knew better and were not convinced to try again.[15] This time, Embury-Martin was gone, and it would not be rebuilt. With the destruction of this mill also came a very visible sign that the end of the lumbering era was indeed reality. All the big mills were gone, and with it, Cheboygan's early prosperity. Over eighty years of sawmills cutting and selling prime northern Michigan lumber became as legendary as the vast forests that once covered the area.

By the end of the 1920s Cheboygan was in a particularly bad situation. Although tourism was finally beginning to increase, the Great Depression was beginning to set in, and with the lumber industry all but eliminated, there were steadily decreasing numbers of jobs to be had. Things got markedly worse in June of 1930. On Monday, 9 June, National Bank examiner Henry F. Quinn came to town to examine the First National Bank's books, as was a common practice for federally chartered National Banks. That afternoon the receiving teller of the bank, Clyde Milliken, left early and went home. The next morning he was found dead in his garage, seated in his car, a revolver from the bank and mirror by his side.

Tuesday morning it was clear why Milliken took his own life. Quinn, in examining the bank's books, discovered that there was a deficit of some $308,000 (adjusted for inflation this amounts to over 3.3 million dollars today). The board of directors had little choice but to suspend operations.[16] A statement from the bank explained the situation.

> The First National Bank closed its doors this morning by resolution of the Directors. Shortages have been found in the accounts of Clyde Milliken, deceased Savings teller of the bank which have seriously affected the bank's financial position.... The First National Bank for 50 years has been considered the soundest institution of its character in Northern Michigan, and one of which the community took great pride. Its closing is a severe blow to Cheboygan. No blame can be attached to anyone with the institution for this shortage except the deceased employe [sic]. The officers and employes of the bank are assisting in all possible ways in working the matter out, and

it is hoped that depositors will be paid 100 cents on the
dollar.[17]

The closing was indeed a severe blow to Cheboygan and the whole area
as well. The loss of such an institution in the community, a prominent
financial pillar, did significant economic harm to Cheboygan's financial
stability.

A portion of a letter dated 15 June 1930 to M.D. Olds from some
friends in Tacoma, Washington, provides a perfect summation of the
unfortunate situation in Cheboygan.

> We were all very shocked to read in the Tacoma paper the news
> of Clyde Milliken's suicide and of the shortage in the bank's
> funds. The item we saw stated that he was short about
> $308,000.00 but we are all inclined to believe that the amount
> has been exaggerated. How could he possibly get away with that
> much money in such a small bank? I know he must have taken
> bonds or other securities in order to get any amount at all but
> would they have that much on hand in negotiable securities...?
> That amount would just about ruin the old town. I never in my
> life saw or heard of a place so absolutely jinxed as that town is. I
> suppose the depositors will suffer considerably if the loss is that
> large... Was Clyde playing the market and did he do the stealing
> over a period of years or all of it just recently? I cannot help but
> feel very sorry for him because he was a pretty good friend of
> mine and a fine fellow. His poor wife must be almost out of her
> mind. It is just too bad and it seems so damn useless because he
> had been getting along alright. I suppose he wanted to be a
> millionaire in a hurry and like every other fool that ever tried it,
> he thought he could get away with it.[18]

This letter illustrates how not only did Cheboygan lose a financial
institution, it lost a friend as well. It is as if the town lost some of its
innocence too – a scandal involving a man who was apparently
respected was now dead and a community in financial turmoil. The
closing of the First National Bank, though not unique among banks

during the depression, was a shock to Cheboygan that had an emotional impact as much as it did a financial one. But all was not lost. Out of the ashes the following year rose the Citizens National Bank, a reputable and secure institution which operates to this day.

While not every town suffered an upset like Cheboygan did with the failure of the First National Bank, others were lamenting the decline of the lumber industry in Michigan. Throughout the state, other lumbering towns were struggling with the notion that soon most of the lumber would be gone. Because it could easily be exhausted if harvested heavily, as it was in Michigan, those communities at its mercy had to face this unfortunate reality. The following table shows the state-wide decline of lumber production throughout Michigan.

REPORTED TIMBER PRODUCTION IN MICHIGAN FOR SELECTED YEARS
MEASUREMENTS IN THOUSAND BOARD FEET (M)

1869	2,251,613
1879	4,178,610
1889	5,478,358
1899	3,018,338
1905	1,719,687
1910	1,681,081
1915	1,032,154
1920	726,147
1925	797,610
1930	466,831
1935	332,700

SOURCE: Compiled from *Lumber Production in the United States, 1799-1946* (Washington, DC: GPO, 1948), pp. 11-17.

It is interesting to note that around the same time the lumber industry began to decline in earnest statewide, it began to do so in the Cheboygan area as well. This indicates a number of things. Cheboygan was at the tail end of the lumber boom in Michigan. Starting in the Saginaw Valley (central Michigan), the forest regions which were harvested gradually made a steady progression north. Although the Upper Peninsula was still farther north than Cheboygan, lumbering interests in Wisconsin often cut timber there, which meant these natural resources did not go to help Michigan's economy. Additionally, much of the lumber in the eastern Upper Peninsula had already been harvested. Much of it was rafted down to be processed further south in places like Cheboygan, in order to keep the mills there running longer. The result is that while there were plenty of other mills still operating throughout the state, including the Upper Peninsula, Cheboygan seems to have been on the forefront of the statewide economic picture, at least as far as lumber was concerned. In consequence, when the industry began to gasp and choke as it was dying, the once thriving city on the Straits fell ill with it.

With the exhaustion of lumber, things had gotten very bad for Cheboygan. Amid dwindling jobs and the consequential vexatious financial predicament, for most there was no reason to stay in town. Sure, it is a beautiful area, but to a working man with a wife and kids, pristine water and fresh air does not put food on the table. Dr. J.M. Cain, a dentist in Cheboygan during the good times and bad, explained what had happened.

> We lost the sawmills, and a big tannery and the paper mill, and every other man seemed to be leaving to work for Ford or Buick. Nobody had any money. Things got so bad that we couldn't raise taxes enough to electrify the water works, which would have meant a big annual saving of outlay, and had to turn the plant over to the power company.[19]

Thankfully, an industrial boom after the Second World War provided some jobs for those people still living in Cheboygan. At the same time this laid the groundwork for revitalization. While slow and steady growth did eventually become the norm, it was at times extremely slow: the county-wide population increased by just eighty-seven people in the period between 1940 and 1950. Northern Michigan, however, would never experience a boom in growth, industrialization or economy like it did during the lumber boom.

The icon of the age, M.D. Olds, had seen Cheboygan at its best and its worst. When he first arrived on the scene, it was the peak of the lumber boom. By now it was something only to reminisce about. He had had a wonderfully successful career as a lumber baron and been an integral part of the community. But even Olds, who was always a forceful negotiator, could not talk his way out of going home to his eternal reward. M.D. Olds quietly passed away from acute hemolytic jaundice at Grayling, Michigan, on 8 September 1935, at age seventy-five. During his life he was a great benefactor to a wide variety of people and organizations. He donated to every church in town. As the *Cheboygan Daily Tribune* reported, "He loaned money to many with no thought of ever being repaid. In scores of other cases he assisted individuals and families in need whenever he could be of assistance. He was genuinely interested in Cheboygan and its welfare." All of this, meanwhile, was often done anonymously and he never sought attention for his generosity.[20] He was buried in the family plot in Cheboygan, not leaving the town where he made his fortune but where he had been occasionally feared, often admired, and always respected.

The death of M.D. Olds was in effect the end of the age in Cheboygan. The last great timber mills and lumber barons were now gone, and the city was no longer a lumbering boom town full of transients and vagabonds. The rough-and-tough shanty boys were a thing of the past, as were log booms, lathe mills and logging trains. That which gave rise to a bustling city was now a scarce commodity, and Cheboygan was left in the difficult position of discovering exactly what its purpose as a city was. Would it be manufacturing, farming or perhaps tourism? It was a confusing time for the community. The county went from ninety-six manufacturing establishments in 1900 to eight by 1940 – precisely one more than it had in 1860, some *eighty years prior.*[21]

As manufacturing jobs became scarcer, farming became a viable way of life for those lucky enough to find adequate land. Despite the population decline which occurred with the end of the lumber boom, the number of farms countywide did not similarly decrease. This did not mean that people were necessarily well off, however. While there was and is plenty of good land in the county, rarely was it as good as it was billed. Lumber companies often drummed up the quality and farming potential of the lands they owned. Once the timber was gone, they would often sell that property as prime farmland, whether it was or not. If they were lucky, the new owners could farm enough to get by or perhaps sell their goods. Sadly, poverty became an all but common reality for many in the area. It was a difficult situation, and something clearly had to be done.

But for those chose to stay, life itself did not necessarily become worse. The area was still rich with natural beauty, providing a welcome respite for whatever may be causing someone physical or emotional ails. As parts of southern Michigan experienced its growth from the auto industry, and as those automobiles made people more mobile, going "up north" became a popular way to spend the weekend or a vacation. Good, urban factory jobs provided people with steady income and vacation time, many of whom chose to utilize the north's resources for their rejuvenation. The lakes and rivers were available for boating or fishing, and sightseeing, hunting, and Cheboygan's excellent proximity to other destinations all made the region agreeable to tourist accommodation.

Despite all of this the differences between the two eras are staggering. In terms of jobs, population growth, and economic productivity, nothing in Cheboygan's recent history (post-1930) can compare with the circumstances which gave rise to the city. Change may be inevitable and although it is not always good, at the very least it contributes to a more interesting and diverse history. Today, after decades of stagnation, Cheboygan is finally headed in the right direction. The 6 July 1946 edition of *The Saturday Evening Post* dubbed Cheboygan "the town that refused to die," and this is true now more than ever.[22] Although there will never be a rapid population explosion like once occurred, signs indicate that the number of people in Cheboygan will continue to increase. A more stable growth, slow and steady rather than rapid, is unlikely to result in a near fifty percent population decline as once happened. There is now continual growth nearly every year, both in terms of population and new businesses. Consequently, Cheboygan will not suffer the same fate that Duncan City did. Unlike the latter, this history is not yet done – Cheboygan's story continues.

7

Remnants of a Bygone Era

Today little remains of what once so gloriously built up the thriving northern communities of Cheboygan and Duncan City. An era marked by capital, manufacturing, transportation and manpower lives on now only in a few scattered buildings, decomposing ruins, and stories of a time not so long ago. Regrettably, the boom and bust of lumber has left little for us today to remember it by. In the early days of the area, the main motivation was profit making, not only by the lumber barons but by those who worked for them as well. Work was seasonal, and profit was king. There was little need to strive for permanency, because after Cheboygan's lumber was all gone, it would be time to move on to some other boom town somewhere else. It was not until later that more and more people began to see themselves as permanent Cheboyganites, but even then there was little consideration of preservation of historically significant buildings or places. If something stood in the way of progress, or it could be used somewhere else, down it came. The magnificent residence of M.D. Olds is but one example, a mansion by any definition that was destroyed to make way for a warehouse. Fires were also exceedingly common, and as we have seen, many landmarks were lost to its destructive fury.

But not everything is gone. Here and there are scattered shells and foundations of the area's glory days. Some of the remnants are physical remains, some are in the stories handed down from one generation to the next, and some are present in legends of questionable authenticity. In each of these examples, the past lives on in the present. Visiting the sites where lumbering operations took place can be a surreal experience if one allows themselves the luxury of slipping back in time to an era which so dramatically and permanently changed this little corner of the world.

An excursion to one of these places can be had by heading down Duncan Avenue towards what used to be the village of Duncan City. At the terminus of the road there is virtually no sign that there was ever anything there other than residences. Now built up with modern homes, signs of the past are gone. Old roads no longer exist, and new subdivisions have been built up. One would never imagine that there was ever much of anything here, let alone a seat of local government, a post office, and a thriving mill with hundreds of employees. The area is completely residential today. Despite the beautiful homes, there is a certain sadness in the air. What once was the area's first permanent village now shows no signs of that prosperity. The entire area which once represented the future of northern Michigan now has nothing to show for it. Thankfully, however, the place where Duncan City once stood is now well-kept and makes a beautiful location to call home. But in the gentle breeze blowing off the lake you can still hear the sawmills running and lumber being hurriedly stacked on the docks. You can smell the sawdust in the air and feel the presence of passengers who so long ago disembarked at this important northern outpost.

Closely linked to what used to be Duncan City, just to the east of this place are the remains of the Cheboygan Main Light Station, the area's first lighthouse. The original light, which was replaced in 1859, continued to operate until 1930. At that time a new fourteen-foot offshore lighthouse was constructed, and the lighthouse was abandoned. In the 1940s the buildings were dismantled. Despite its prominent location, eventually the light was replaced and Cheboygan Main became little more than an abandoned and forgotten relic site.

Despite the fact that the buildings are gone, there are still a considerable number of remains. Large sections of the foundation of the light keeper's residence are still in place, as are pieces of the old light tower, which at one time provided a safe beacon for those ships making their way to the booming communities of Cheboygan and Duncan City. Scattered bricks which once made up these structures litter the ground. But perhaps most eerily of all is the original sidewalk. While it is in a gradually deteriorating condition, it remains quite usable and provides a path from the lighthouse ruins to the beach and a breathtaking view of the Straits of Mackinac. Pause here long enough and one can imagine the ghosts of keepers past walking past you, making their way out to the beach to see a vessel sailing into Jeremiah Duncan's mill, or perhaps coming from Embury-Martin, loaded up and carrying with it a fresh cut of prime northern Michigan pine.

The Cheboygan Main Light Station today, located in Cheboygan State Park.

A few miles to the west are more visible signs. In downtown Cheboygan, along the river, an occasional old log still sticks its head out of the water. But just outside of town there is a much more visible relic to be seen. On the shore of Lake Huron just off Mackinaw Avenue lie the remains of the once prosperous Embury-Martin Lumber Company.

Today, the ruins of the Embury-Martin Company provide a powerful witness to this era. A trip here immediately causes the visitor to imagine the countless millions of board feet of lumber which were once cut here, neatly stacked and sitting on the docks and tramway. (At the time of the aforementioned fire there were an estimated five million feet of lumber stacked on the tramway, although this went undamaged).[1] The weeds which have grown up shadow the greater glory of the old mill as one tries to imagine the immensity of the operations which once occurred here. Remains of the docks jetting far into the lake challenge one to imagine ships being loaded up, the mill loudly ravishing countless logs, day and night, night and day. The purring engines, the newly piled lumber, the smell of freshly-cut wood and the sight of steam from the boiler mixed with the deep, dark blue of a clear summer morning would have been an amazing spectacle for the senses.

Walking the grounds, one can easily find driftwood and a few lingering uncut logs, as well as old metal pipes and fragments of glass and burned wood. Bits of coal also litter the ground, some of it likely burned to fuel the engines of a mill and a city. Wading through chest high weeds, the seeker can find where the pump house, machine shop and blacksmith's shop all once were. The foundations are long gone, now replaced with mere indentations in the ground and an occasional piece of well-disintegrated cement. Pilings of various height shoot up from the lakebed and shore, their docks which at one time would have been capable of holding millions of feet of lumber now completely destroyed and carried away, the remains being shown little mercy by time and the seasons.

Little remains of the mill itself. Only the walls and chimney of the boiler room remain standing.[2] The towering concrete mass is a fascinating monument to the permanence of the lumbering era on Cheboygan's development. Looking at the whole of what used to be, the scattered and broken concrete structures, the waste piles, the remains of hundreds of feet of dockage, and the visitor to Embury-Martin today cannot help but be struck at how quiet this once booming place now is.

One piece of Cheboygan's early history, despite its fair share of setbacks, has withstood the test of time and remains as valuable now as it was then. An anchor of the downtown community and vital piece of it, the Opera House continues to be "the focal point for entertainment and the performing arts in the Straits of Mackinac area and beyond."

Remains of the Embury-Martin Lumber Company.

After falling into disuse and disrepair, it was reopened in 1984 after a lengthy restoration. Today, the Victorian-themed arts facility presents concerts, stage productions, comedians, and others to all of northern Michigan. Despite being destroyed or damaged twice by fire and nearly decimated by decay, the building today is a lasting remnant of the lumber era that has not suffered the same fate as so many other buildings did in the traumatic final years of that period.[3]

There is at least one other physical remnant of the era which persists in local folklore but as yet has failed to materialize. A local legend tells the story of the lost locomotive of Cheboygan. Sometime around 1915, the story goes, a man in the employ of M.D. Olds named Charles Martineau was operating one of his large wood-hauling locomotives (similar to the type used by Embury-Martin, the aptly named "Pulpwood Special"). For whatever reason, Martineau and his boss had a significant difference of opinion, and the former, in a fit of rage, drove the engine into a swampy mess. The giant machine quickly became caught in the abyss of mud, weeds and slime, and the beast of burden was lost, stuck in the swampy woods, never to be recovered. Time passed, weeds grew up, trees reappeared, and the engine became part of the local landscape.

Decades later, it appears that the engine may be gone forever, if it was ever out there at all. Many people have claimed to have seen it, although no one has ever produced a single photograph or been able to retrace their steps to where the Olds locomotive supposedly is. Granted, if it is out there, it would be incredibly difficult to find. The conditions are more unforgiving now then they were at the time the contraption was lost. What is more, the engine has had plenty of time to sink and become overgrown with weeds, trees, vines, moss, or any other variety of shrubbery and timber. The supposed location is widely known as being somewhere off of the Alpena State Road, just east of town and off of the old railroad grade. Hunters, snowmobilers, and those just roaming in the woods have supposedly seen it. The Department of Natural Resources, private searchers in airplanes, salvagers, and of course historians have all made the trek out to where the locomotive could or should be located.[4] All of the searches have as of yet been fruitless.

Although the location is not known exactly, it may have been at one point. The engine could have been scrapped by someone who just happened to stumble across it, especially during the World War II years. A good deal of the supposed sightings took place well after the war, however, so whatever is true is anybody's guess. Another possibility is that the machine may have by this point sunk so far into the swamp it could not ever be seen. In any event, what is true without a doubt is that the story refuses to go away, partly because so many people claim to have seen the engine, but also because it is a fun story to retell.

But there is a possibility that this story is exactly that – a story. Tales of locomotives lost in the woods are not unique, even in northern Michigan. Like the tales of the mighty Paul Bunyan, it may just be that there is no locomotive off of Alpena State Road at all.

On the sides of the old rights-of-way, hunters often find rotting ties, rusted spikes, perhaps even a coupling. These mementos fuel one of the north country's most enduring folk legends. For over beer are exchanged rumors of vintage locomotives stranded in cedar swamps, iron horses sidetracked a generation ago, forgotten and now left rusting in the forest. Like the Sasquatch and the hodag, these phantom locomotives are often discussed, occasionally sought out, but never found.[5]

Indeed this seems to be the persistent problem, that no one has yet (locally, anyway) proven the existence of any one of these machines. As one historian has suggested, "Despite a lack of proof, the stories of lost logging era locomotives linger, in part because of the desire of the people who live on the fringe of the forest to have a more direct contact with their community's golden past."[6] This assertion makes sense. A story such as the lost Olds locomotive ties the present to the past, linking a more romantic time to the reality of the present, still clutching a relic of a bygone age.

On the other hand, there are examples where stories of lost locomotives in the woods have proven to be more than just nostalgic fairy-tales. In some very rare cases (notably in British Columbia), these machines have been located and photographs taken, proving their existence. It is known for a fact that Charles Martineau was indeed in the employ of Olds at one time, thus at least some details of the story seem credible.[7] But in the far majority of cases there is no solid evidence, or the "locomotive" that is found is confused for some other large piece of machinery. In countless stories in logging communities across North America, locomotives have been lost because they have fallen through the ice, slipped off their grade, or been the victim of some other unfortunate circumstances. Rarely do these tales amount to anything other than a fireside narrative.

The terrain today is no more developed now than it was when the machine was supposedly lost. The sandy soil occasionally gives way to lower points in the topography, in which have grown any number of weeds, blackberry bushes and small trees. In lower places, remains of the old railroad grade can still be seen, built up paths now long since abandoned. These places are particularly striking. To know that along these paths once rumbled Olds' locomotive as it carried away thousands of logs, en route to his mill, provides anyone looking at them a very real image that the growth and development of the area stretched out here to this now quiet, tranquil land.

Following the road, one can see some of the swampy regions which dot the countryside, any one of which could hold the missing locomotive. These swampy regions are devoid of trees, of course, but plenty of lofty weeds grow in the dark, thick mud. Any vehicle driven too far into this nefarious ooze would likely be stuck forever. Locating the engine, then, would be like trying to find a needle in a sawdust pile.

Maybe it is out there after all. Lots of details are "known," including the name of the engineer who supposedly ran it into the swamp, Charles Martineau. But because no one has ever produced a shred of evidence to the contrary, it is likely the story of the Olds locomotive lost so many years ago is nothing more than a relic of the past in and of itself. Even if it is just a story, it nevertheless is an artifact of a glorious era which provided plenty of opportunities in which it could have been true. And if that story helps people remember who they were then, are now, and see where they want to go, then that is much more important than finding a rusting metal hulk.

*　　　　　　*　　　　　　*

For the entire Cheboygan region during its time as a lumber "boom town," it has been estimated that well over a billion board feet of wood were cut, with some estimates approaching two billion. As a direct result of this, Cheboygan and the area grew from an isolated and virtually non-existent rural community to a thriving industrial center and, to a certain extent, back again. But decades after the demise of the lumber industry, the struggling community gradually became again a place of tourism and limited manufacturing. What comes out of Cheboygan today does not resemble that which was produced in the 1890s, but then again it was impossible for that type of industry to be sustainable for long. For those who stayed and adapted to the new northern Michigan economy, they did not find a straight and smooth road in front of them. Rather, they had to adapt, and thankfully they did. Today Cheboygan is nowhere near its population zenith of about 7,000 in the 1890s, but well over 5,000 still live and work there. A significant amount of manufacturing and professional jobs are still present and, ironically enough, there are even a few timber harvesters.

Why Cheboygan did not become more than it did after the collapse of the lumber industry hinges upon a number of factors. From a very early point in its history, Cheboygan's pioneers set a course for her, explaining the necessary requirements for a lasting and permanent city. The inaugural issue of the *Northern Tribune*, 17 July 1875, details some of these prerequisites:

> The growth of a city is very similar to the growth of any business enterprise. First there must be the need of a city. The growing resources of the country must demand one. This, Cheboygan possesses to an extent excelled by few places. Second, it must first have enterprising, energetic business men, men who, at the same time that they labor for the advancement of their own interests, will labor for the general advancement of the place. Third, the representatives of the business place must, while they may not abate their business competition, work together like different members of a mercantile firm, for the advancement, for the growth, for the prosperity of their city.

There can be no doubt that there was a need for the city of Cheboygan. America was growing, and so the resources of northern Michigan were in heavy demand. Secondly, Cheboygan was not at all short of businessmen who were willing and able to rise to the occasion and establish their mills, yards, stores and hotels. Collectively it could be argued that they were working for the general advancement of the place. Hotels could not operate without tourists and businessmen, businessmen could not operate if they could not see the area before they established their businesses, residents would not move somewhere were there were no businesses, and stores could not operate where there were no residents. The entire settling of a community is a completely cyclical process in the long-term, overarching view, although at an intra-city level it may not necessarily appear so.

A significant question is posed by the third requirement, that is, did Cheboygan's early proprietors "work together like different members of a mercantile firm, for the advancement, for the growth, for the prosperity of their city"? To this there is no easy answer. While all of the lumber barons were clearly competing against each other, and the sheer number of lumber companies can attest to this fact, one cannot easily say that rivalries or cutthroat competition for profits were the reason that Cheboygan's growth ceased and reversed. To the contrary, there is reason to believe that at least some of the lumber barons got along well with each other and that their families often associated together.[8] The ultimate reason for the rapid decline in Cheboygan's status as a prominent lumbering town lies in the fact that the lumber was needed so badly, so quickly, that it made sense to hurriedly set up in Cheboygan, cut lumber for a few years, and then move on when it ran out or something more profitable came along. So long as there was need for this lumber (and it was available), there was the need for the companies, stores, and homes, and so the city. But when the lumber ran out, there was little reason left to stay. Sure, other business did gradually take off and some even continue to this day, but when the real catalyst of lumber was exhausted, there was nothing left to fuel the fire of growth. Even if the lumber barons and other proprietors had worked more closely together, it is unlikely Cheboygan's growth would have continued long after the peak production years of the mid-1890s.

The State of Michigan during its prime years as a lumber producing region, until about 1900, manufactured a total of 160 billion board feet. Its value was better than two and half billion dollars, over a billion dollars more than all of the gold that came out of California in the same period. The total value of the pine harvested in Michigan is more than ten times the gold taken out of Alaska and three times that in California.[9] While staggering amounts of lumber were coming from the lower regions of the state, the north was also producing its fair share. Often overshadowed by events downstate, northern Michigan too had its impact, which often goes unacknowledged. Places like Grand Rapids and Saginaw were important in their own right, but the north also deserves its due accreditation. Cheboygan's pioneers contributed in a very significant way to not only building up northern Michigan, but also to the overall well-being and financial stability of the state. The economic revenue generated by the lumber industry, in which

Cheboygan played a pivotal and significant part, helped make Michigan the manufacturing and recreational hub it is today. Ignoring the contributions of northern towns and cities like Cheboygan, Traverse City, Petoskey, and St. Ignace is doing a great disservice to the greater history of Michigan. Without their input from the lumber era, not only would they not exist, but Michigan's economy would have developed much more slowly.

In 1872 the editor of *The Lumberman's Gazette*, C.B. Headley, quoted the words of the Rev. C.H. Bingham. In a prediction of the future of northern Michigan, the gentlemen expressed their mutual opinion.

> The pioneer is insensible to arguments touching the future supply of timber; to him the forest is only fit to be exterminated, as it hinders his plow and obstructs his sunlight. When northern Michigan becomes like southern Illinois, a great rolling prairie of grass and grain, whose horizon is as unbroken as the horizon of the ocean, the want of foresight that permitted the destruction of these magnificent forests will be bitterly lamented.[10]

In post-boom Cheboygan, one could have made the argument that if northern Michigan did look like southern Illinois, maybe that would not be such a bad thing – at least there would have been plenty of harvestable crops and jobs. The early pioneers of the area perhaps did not look at the land and its resources as they should have. Their lack of foresight precluded later economic growth. But to their credit, one must remember that the whole objective of living on the frontier, and then in more organized settlements, is providing an economic means for survival. The pioneers of old did not have the hindsight to which we are privy. One cannot forget that had their ventures never brought them north, our sturdy pioneers would never have settled the area and there would not be nearly the number of northern towns and cities as there are today. But even more importantly, the economic benefits would never have been realized and the statewide economy would not have been nearly what it was and is. As Michigan and the nation grew, regionalized economic growth was quintessential to their success. In this way even a regional boom can have a much greater effect than is immediately evident. Throughout the country, similar circumstances occurred in any number of places, and each impacted the overall growth of the United States. In some cases the communities evaporated after the boom; but in others, they stuck around. Cheboygan, thankfully, did the latter.

Today the city continues, albeit at its now slower pace, to expand. Most recently a hospital expansion, construction projects downtown, and the building of new schools indicate that there is still life in this community, and good reason to hope for the future. Despite the fact that Cheboygan was clearly founded as a lumbering community, she has decided to stay. There are unquestionably challenges which its residents must face, questions that the sturdy pioneers thankfully did not have to answer. Nevertheless, in their spirit her citizens strive on to make the community welcoming, productive and beautiful. The lumbering heydays may be long past, but the city of Cheboygan, which those days gave rise to, remains. Its heritage is an integral part of the present, and with knowledge of this, there is no reason why its future cannot be any less celebrated than its past.

Appendix

Notes

Appendix A: Cheboygan County Communities Past and Present

When moving into a new area, newcomers often settle in groups of varying contiguousness. They do this for any one of a variety of reasons: for mutual support and protection, proximity to transportation, geographic / agricultural conditions, or for just about any number of other rationale. Sometimes, through the course of cultural and societal evolution, these towns prosper and flourish. Other times they die out. The following list presents every known named settlement (or what passes as a settlement) in Cheboygan County, from its inception to the present day, modern subdivisions excluded. Those places marked with an asterisk (*) are known to have or have had a post office. Alternative names for settlements are given in parentheses. Very little, indeed in some cases virtually nothing, are known about some of these communities. As discussed previously, many were no more than stops on the railroads or lumber "loading areas." Whatever the case may be, each one adds to the legacy and rich history of northern Michigan.

Cheboygan County Cities, Towns, Villages and Settlements, 1840 – Present

Afton* (Ellisville)

Alverno* (Black River, St. Joseph, Sova*)

Ball*

Bryants (Douglas Lake)

Buckhorn

Cheboygan* (West Duncan)

Cornwell*

Duncan* (Duncan City)

Forest Home

Geyersville*

Haakwood*

Hebron*

Aloha*

Armstrong

Birchwood

Burt Lake* (Buckeye Resort)

Bushville

Churchill

Dow*

Fingerboard Corners

Freedom*

Gilchrist

Hamby

Indianville (Pokagon's Village)

Indian River*	Ingleside*
Inverness	Koehler*
Lake Side	Lake Wood
La Grand	LeGrand* (Ostrander Station)
Longpoint*	Manning*
Mackinaw City* (Mackinaw*)	Mentor*
Millers	Milliken*
Mullet Lake*	Ohioville
Riggsville*	Rondo*
Sand Pit	Smith's Mill
Steinhof	Taft
Topinabee*	Tower*
Trowbridge*	Watsonville
Waveland	Weadock*
Wildwood*	Wolverine* (Torrey)
Wolverine Switch	Youngs

SOURCE: Compiled from "Cheboygan County," The Traverse Region, Historical and Descriptive, Illustrated, 104; Gordon Turner, Pioneering North: Historical Highlights of the Cheboygan Era; Meyers, P.A and J.A. Meyers, Plat Book of Cheboygan County, Michigan; and various contemporary and modern maps, ca. 1895-2005.

Appendix B: A Legislative History of Cheboygan

The formal creation of any village, town, city, county, or other civil community cannot occur without the proper legislative authority. A process of considerable complexity, bills and laws had to be passed through the state legislature (then as now) to allow for the "official" recognition of a settlement. Here are reproduced verbatim all of the relevant laws which allowed the city and county of Cheboygan to be organized. Several changes had to be made throughout the early history of both; however, by the beginning of the 1890s, the county had been created as it exists now and the city had also been created (subsequent additions to the city would cause it to grow substantially in size from when it was first chartered in 1889). This section of the appendix is intended to provide the reader with a brief history of how, as a matter of legislative technicality, Cheboygan County and City were created.

In Public Law No. 119 of the year 1840, the State of Michigan provided for the creation of thirty-five counties within Michigan, one of which was Cheboygan. In this law, the county was created about half of the size it is today. The southern portion was the county of Wyandot.

AN ACT to lay off and define the boundaries of certain counties.

Be it enacted by the Senate and House of Representatives of the State of Michigan...

SECTION 26. That portion of the state embraced in towns thirty-three, thirty-four, thirty-five and thirty-six north, of ranges one east, and one, two and three west, shall be laid off as a separate county, to be known and designated as the county of Wyandot.

SEC. 29. That portion of the state lying north of the line between towns thirty-six and thirty-seven north, and east of the line between ranges four and five west shall be laid off as a separate county, to be known and designated as the county of Cheboygan.

Approved, April 1, 1840.

A mere dozen years after the creation of the State of Michigan, Public Law No. 84 of 1849 provided for the creation of several townships all over the state, including that of "Sheboygan," a remote region far to the north of the capital. Strangely, it specified the creation of the township in the County of Sheboygan. In actuality, there was no such county, nor had there ever been. Despite the error in recording the name, the law held, and the township was created. Only the sections relevant to this study are reproduced here.

AN ACT to organize certain townships, and for other purposes.

Be it enacted by the Senate and House of Representatives of the State of Michigan...

SECTION 10. That all that part of the state of Michigan, known as the county of Cheboygan, and now attached to the township of Holmes in the county of Mackinac, shall be set off from said township and organized into a separate township by the name of Sheboygan, and the first township meeting therein, shall be held at the house of Jacob Sammons, in said township.

SEC. 17. All acts and parts of acts contravening any of the provisions of this act be, and the same hereby are repealed.

SEC. 18. This act shall take effect and be in force from and after its passage.

Approved March 15, 1849.

By 1853 the state legislature deemed it necessary to combine the counties of Cheboygan and Wyandot, which they did with Public Law No. 20.

AN ACT to organize the county of Cheboygan.

SECTION 1. The people of the state of Michigan enact, That the counties of Cheboygan and Wyandot shall be organized in one county, by the name of Cheboygan, and the inhabitants thereof entitled to all the rights, privileges, and immunities to which by law the inhabitants of other organized counties are entitled.

SEC. 2. There shall be elected in the county of Cheboygan, on the first Tuesday of May next, all the several county officers to which by law the said county is entitled, and the said election and the canvass shall, in all respects, be conducted and held in the manner prescribed by law for holding elections and canvasses for county and state officers: Provided, That the canvass shall be held in the village of Duncan, in said county, on the Monday next following said election; and said county officers shall be immediately qualified and enter upon the duties of their respective offices, and their several terms of office shall expire at the same time they would have expired had they been elected at the last general election: And provided further, That until such county officers are elected and qualified, the proper officers of the county of Mackinac shall perform all the duties appertaining to the officers of said county of Cheboygan, in the same manner as though this act had not passed.

SEC. 3. The board of canvassers of said county, under this act, shall consist of the presiding inspector of each township therein, who shall organize by appointing one of their number chairman, and another secretary of the board, and shall thereupon proceed to discharge all the duties of a board of county canvassers, as in ordinary cases of elections for county and state officers.

SEC. 4. The county of Cheboygan shall have concurrent jurisdiction upon Lake Huron, and Thunder and Saginaw Bays, with the other counties contiguous thereto.

SEC. 5. All that part of the township of Cheboygan which lies west of the middle of the main channel of Mullet Lake, and Cheboygan River, and of a line extended due north from the mouth of said river to the north bounds of the county, shall be organized into a separate township, by the name of Duncan, and the first township meeting therein shall be held at the hotel in the village of Duncan.

SEC. 6. The county seat of Cheboygan County is hereby fixed and established at the village of Duncan, on Cheboygan River, in said county.

SEC. 7. The counties of Presque Isle, Alpena, Montmorency, Otsego, Crawford, Oscoda, Alcona, Iosco, Ogemaw, and Roscommon are hereby attached to the county of Cheboygan for judicial and municipal purposes.

SEC. 8. This act shall take effect immediately.

Approved Jan. 29, 1853.

Pursuant to the recently-enacted legislation, the first election in the redrawn county was held on 1 May 1853. In the following list are compiled Cheboygan County's first elected public officials.

County Clerk – James S. Douglass
Register of Deeds – Hiram A. Rood
Judge of Probate – Bela Chapman
Sheriff – Medard Metivier
County Treasurer – Bela Chapman
Prosecuting Attorney – Samuel H. Price
Circuit Court Commissioner – Samuel H. Price
County Surveyor – Hiram L. Burr
Coroners – Richard Knight, Lorin P. Riggs
Fish Inspector – Daniel L. Strang

It would take the better part of two decades before the village of Cheboygan was officially created. This was done in 1871 with Public Law 284. In the interest of brevity, only the first and last sections shall be reproduced here.

AN ACT to incorporate the village of Cheboygan.

SECTION 1. The People of the State of Michigan enact, That fractional section twenty-nine, thirty, thirty-one, and thirty-two, in fractional township number thirty-eight north, of range number one west, be and the same is hereby constituted a village corporate, under the name of the village of Cheboygan.

SEC. 30. This act shall take immediate effect.

Approved April 17, 1871.

A few years later the village of Cheboygan was reincorporated under Local Act No. 278 of 1877, approved 27 March of that year. Essentially, it provided for the continuation of the village of Cheboygan as it was, with provisions being made exempting the village from any obligation to "…keep in repair any of the bridges now constructed or hereafter to be constructed across the Cheboygan river within the limits of said village…." The responsibility of maintaining the bridges now fell to the township as it existed before the village was created. Prior to this, bridge responsibilities fell to the village and township collectively.

The City of Cheboygan was finally incorporated in 1889 with Local Act No. 333 of that year. Again, in the interest of pithiness, only the first section shall be reproduced.

AN ACT to incorporate the city of Cheboygan and to repeal an act entitled, "An act to re-incorporate the village of Cheboygan in the County of Cheboygan," approved March twenty-seven, one thousand eight hundred and seventy-seven.

SECTION 1: The People of the State of Michigan enact, That the following territory, to wit: Fractional sections nineteen, twenty-eight, twenty-nine, thirty and thirty-one; sections thirty-two and thirty-three, all in town thirty-eight north, of range one west; all lying east of the north and south quarter line in fractional section twenty-four, and the east half of sections twenty-five and twenty-six, in town thirty-eight north, of range two west; the northeast quarter of section one in town thirty-seven north, of range two west; the north half of sections four, five and six, in town thirty-seven north, of range one west; all lying and being in the county of Cheboygan and State of Michigan (including the present organized village of Cheboygan), be and the same is hereby set off and detached from the townships of Benton, Beaugrand and Inverness, in said county, as now organized, and erected into and declared to be a city by the name of the city of Cheboygan, by which name it shall hereafter be known: Provided, however, That until the fourth day of July, eighteen hundred and eighty-nine, and no longer, the territory hereby set off from the township of Benton shall, for judicial purposes, and for such purposes only, be and remain attached to, and continue to form a part of said township.

This act is ordered to take immediate effect.
Approved March 13, 1889.

With the incorporation of the City of Cheboygan in 1889, both the county and city had been officially organized.

Appendix C: Religious Groups in the Community

"The nucleus of all commercial business, together with social and religious privileges, have been well and judiciously established, and combines to present healthy growth."

—Cheboygan Business Men's Association, 1898.

The rapid influx of settlers into the Cheboygan area beginning in the latter nineteenth century and continuing throughout the first decade of the next necessitated the development of a number of religious congregations. By 1925 some eighteen different churches had been established in town and in the surrounding area. Although Cheboygan was essentially a frontier town, it is evident from numbers such as this that despite the high numbers of transient workers who clearly did not plan on settling permanently, a significant amount did. Moreover, those that did stay took their religion seriously, enough so that they would gladly organize a church and practice their faith together.

The following table shows each church established in Cheboygan until 1937, with as much relevant information as is known or can be clearly ascertained (two churches in Riggsville are also included because of their proximity and relevance to Cheboygan). First is given the name of the church, the year the first services were held and by whom, and the year a permanent structure was built and who was pastor at the time or responsible for its construction.

Credit should be given to Jesuit missionary Fr. Jacques Marquette, S.J., who arrived in the area in 1671 and was the first person to begin missionary work there.

Religious Groups in the Cheboygan Community, 1852-1937.

Name of Church	Year of first meeting	Founding Pastor	First permanent structure built	Pastor responsible for structure's completion
St. Mary's Catholic	1852	Rev. Patrick Murray	1856	Rev. Patrick Murray
St. Paul's Methodist	1868	Rev. William Riley	1872	Rev. A.I. Wheeler
First Congregational	1871	Rev. John Maile	1874	Rev. John Maile
St. James Episcopal	1872	Rev. Wm. D. Stonex	1879	Rev. W.W. Rafter
First Baptist	1874	"A small group"	1881	Rev. H.A. Conrad
St. John's Lutheran†	1880	Rev. K.A. Otto	ca. 1902	Rev. K.A. Otto
Sacred Heart Catholic†	1881	*	1889	Fr. Leopold Opyrchalski
St. Thomas Lutheran	1881	Rev. K.A. Otto	ca. 1882	Rev. K.A. Otto?

Matthew J. Friday

Name of Church	Year of first meeting	Founding Pastor	First permanent structure built	Pastor responsible for structure's completion
Salvation Army	1889	Capt. Freheit, Corp. Webb	1889	Capt. Freheit
St. Charles Catholic	1895	(From St. Mary's)	1915	Fr. J.B.E. Magnan
St. Lawrence Catholic	1896	(From St. Mary's)	*	Fr. Grochowski, Fr. Casimir Skory
St. John's Evangelical Lutheran	1898	Rev. Henry F. Specken	1903	Rev. M. Nichel
Christian Scientist	1899	‡	1938	‡
Seventh Day Adventist	1917	"A Small Group"	1924	Elder Irving Sheffer
Free Methodist	1925	Rev. E.L. Haywood	1937	Rev. T.H. Reid
Zion Lutheran (Duncan City)	*	*	*	*

* Unknown or not applicable.   † Located in Riggsville.

‡ Interested persons first met at the home of Mrs. Charles Sands; a house was subsequently purchased and converted for use as a church.

SOURCE: Compiled from various primary and secondary sources, newspapers, church archives, and mail surveys.

Chronology, 1778-1935

1778/9 Captain Samuel Robertson temporarily settles at the mouth of the Cheboygan River.

1837   Michigan admitted to the Union as the twenty-sixth state.

1844   Alexander McLeod settles on the Cheboygan River.

1845   Jacob Sammons settles permanently on the Cheboygan River.

1848   Sammons receives title to what would become downtown Cheboygan.

1849   Township of Sheboygan organized.

1851   Village of Cheboygan platted.
Cheboygan Main Light Station constructed.

1852   Jeremiah Duncan purchases property east of the Cheboygan settlement.

1853   Mill construction begins on Duncan's property. The area becomes known as "Duncan" or "Duncan City."

1854   J.W. Duncan dies in Wilmington, Delaware.

1865   McArthur, Southwick and Company organized, predecessor to the W. & A. McArthur Company.

1867   Cheboygan Slack Water Navigation Company organized.

1869   Work completed on the Cheboygan River locks.

1870   Cheboygan's population reaches 800.

1871   Cheboygan organized as a village.
        Congress allocates funds to dredge the Cheboygan River.

1875   St. Mary's Catholic Church (present structure) completed.

1877   Cheboygan reincorporated as a village.

1882   First National Bank of Cheboygan organized.
        W. & A. McArthur Company, Ltd., organized.

1881   Michigan Central Railroad connection established.

1889   Cheboygan incorporated as a city.

1894   Cheboygan's population peaks at 6,957.

1897   Canada places an embargo on sending logs to the United States
        for processing.

1898   The "Big Mill" at Duncan City burns, quickly turning the
        settlement into a ghost town.

1902   W. & A. McArthur Company sold to the American Bag and
        Paper Company.

1904   Millard D. Olds purchases the Nelson & Clark mill (formerly
        the Cheboygan Lumber Company).

1907   Cheboygan Chamber of Commerce begins promoting
        Cheboygan as a tourist destination.

1916   M.D. Olds & Co. ceases operations.

1922   Fire devastates downtown Cheboygan.

1926   Pfister and Vogel Tannery closes.

1928   Embury-Martin Lumber Company destroyed by fire.

1930   First National Bank of Cheboygan permanently suspends
       operations.

1931   Citizens National Bank opens.

1935   Millard D. Olds dies.

Notes

Foreword

[1] Fredrick Jackson Turner, "The Significance of the Frontier in American History," qtd. in *Does the Frontier Experience Make America Exceptional?* Richard W. Etulain, 3, 19.
[2] Ibid., 35.

1. The Historical Prologue

[1] *Manitawauba Chronicle,* 25 March 1871.
[2] *Michigan: Official Directory and Legislative Manual, 1929-1930,* 7.
[3] Bruce A. Rubenstein and Lawrence E. Ziewacz, *Michigan: A History of the GreatLakes State, 3rd ed.,* 49.
[4] Ibid., 67.
[5] The land was not abandoned, but it was not paid to veterans, either; land in Illinois and Missouri was allocated for this purpose instead. Joe Grimm, ed. *Michigan Voices: Our State's History in the Words of the People Who Lived it,* 33.
[6] I am grateful to Dr. Timothy O'Neil for some of the preceding information.
[7] "Cheboygan County," *The Traverse Region, Historical and Descriptive, Illustrated,* 95-96.
[8] Ibid., 96; University of Virginia, *Geostat Center: Historical Census Browser,* "Michigan, Cheboygan County," http://fisher.lib.virginia.edu/collections/stats/histcensus/ (accessed 10 August 2005).
[9] C.B. Headley, "The Pine Forests of Michigan," *The Lumberman's Gazette,* July 1872, 2.
[10] Charles W. Jay, *My New Home in Northern Michigan, and Other Tales* (Trenton, NJ: W.S. and E.A. Sharp, 1874), 36.
[11] Milo M. Quaife, ed. *The John Askin Papers, Vol. 1, 1747-1795* (Detroit: Detroit Library Commission, 1928), 14, 68, 70; Ellis Olson, in correspondence with the author, 5 November 2005.
[12] *Michigan Pioneer and Historical Collections, Vol. 9, (1886), 2nd ed.,* 642-43.

[13] Excepting the Native American presence. Jay's Treaty, signed between the United States and Britain in November 1794 mandated that the British leave all forts on the Great Lakes (including Michilimackinac) by 1 June 1796, thus ending the British occupation of the Straits region.

[14] Ellis Olson, in discussion with the author, 5 November 2005; Perry F. Powers, *A History of Northern Michigan and its People, Vol. 1*, 448.

[15] George Robinson and R.A. Sprague, *History of Cheboygan and Mackinaw Counties*, 18.

[16] Ellis Olson, in conversation with the author, 5 November 2005.

[17] Walter Romig, *Michigan Place Names*, 112.

[18] George N. Fuller, ed. *Historic Michigan: Land of the Great Lakes, Vol. 1*, 474.

[19] Ellis Olson, in conversation with the author, 5 November 2005.

[20] Robinson, *History of Cheboygan and Mackinaw Counties*, 18; Ware, *The Centennial History of Cheboygan County and Village*, 32.

[21] Ware, *The Centennial History*, 33.

[22] General Land Office at Genesee, Michigan, Land Patent to Jacob Sammons dated September 1, 1848, document numbers 2210-2212; Ellis N. Olson, "Historical Development of River," *Cheboygan Centennial 1889-1989*, 29.

[23] Robinson, *History of Cheboygan and Mackinaw Counties*, 19.

[24] "Cheboygan County," *The Traverse Region*, 112.

[25] Barbara E. Benson, *Logs and Lumber: The Development of Lumbering in Michigan's Lower Peninsula, 1837-1870*, 73.

[26] Sr. Marciana, SSJ, ed. *Serving You: Post Offices of Michigan 1802-1976*, 174.

[27] "Cheboygan County," *The Traverse Region*, 109.

[28] The bishop's name was Le Fevre. Ware, *The Centennial History*, 38.

[29] Carol Stempky, *History of the Catholic Church "St. Mary's,"* 11. Bishop Baraga's impact on the Catholic community in Cheboygan, and much of northern Michigan, is profound. He was an extremely devout and well respected missionary, who was successful in his evangelization efforts in the Upper Peninsula as well as in the northern Lower Peninsula. To cite but one example of his abilities, on one Sunday in February, 1860, he preached in French, English and a Native American language (probably Chippewa), and confirmed eighty-two people on the same (see p. 12).

[30] Stempky, *History of the Catholic Church "St. Mary's,"* 15; *Cheboygan Daily Tribune, Golden Jubilee Edition*, 30 June 1939.

[31] "Cheboygan County," *The Traverse Region*, 109; Ware, *The Centennial History*, 57.

[32] Ellis Olson, papers.

[33] Ibid.; *Manitawauba Chronicle*, 25 March 1871.

[34] Robinson, *History of Cheboygan and Mackinaw Counties*, 20; Ware, *The Centennial History*, 36.

[35] Robinson, *History of Cheboygan and Mackinaw Counties*, 20.

[36] General Land Office at Genesee, Michigan, Land Patent to Jeremiah W. Duncan dated February 10, 1852, document number 2804; Robinson, *History of Cheboygan and Mackinaw Counties*, 20.

[37] Gordon Turner, "Ghost Town Once Thrived Nearby," in *Pioneering North: Historical Highlights of the Cheboygan Area*, 9.

[38] Fosimire, "History of Cheboygan," 5; Gordon Turner, "Ghost Town Once Thrived Nearby," in *Pioneering North: Historical Highlights of the Cheboygan Area*, 9.
[39] "Cheboygan County," *The Traverse Region*, 105.
[40] Powers, *A History of Northern Michigan and its People, Vol. 1*, 449.
[41] United States Light-House Board. *List of Light-Houses, Lighted Beacons, and Floating Lights of the United States*, 74-75.
[42] Olson, "Historical Development of River," 31; Ware, *The Centennial History*, 33-34.

2. The Growth of the Community

[1] Olson, "Historical Development of River," 31.
[2] Fosimire, "History of Cheboygan," 6.
[3] *Cheboygan Daily Tribune, Golden Jubilee Edition*, 30 June 1939; *The Manitawauba Chronicle*, 11 March 1871; *The Traverse Region*, 113.
[4] *Cheboygan Daily Tribune, Golden Jubilee Edition*, 30 June 1939.
[5] *The Traverse Region*, 113; *The Northern Tribune*, 11 December 1884.
[6] *Cheboygan Daily Tribune, Golden Jubilee Edition*, 30 June 1939. *The Traverse Region*, 113; Ellis Olson, in conversation with the author, 5 November 2005.
[7] *The Manitawauba Chronicle*, 11 March 1871; Ellis Olson, in conversation with the author, 5 November 2005.
[8] *Cheboygan Daily Tribune, Golden Jubilee Edition*, 30 June 1939; Ware, *The Centennial History*, 45.
[9] *Acts of the Legislature of the State of Michigan, 1861*, 461, 464-5.
[10] *Acts of the Legislature of the State of Michigan, 1869*, 1669-1670; *Local and Personal Acts of the Legislature of the State of Michigan, 1871, Vol. 3*, 1233.
[11] Atwood, "Cheboygan as a Nineteenth Century Lumber Area," 163-4.
[12] M.D. Olds papers, Central Michigan University; *The Traverse Region*, 106.
[13] *The Traverse Region*, 106; Atwood, "Cheboygan as a Nineteenth Century Lumber Area," 55-56; Powers, *A History of Northern Michigan and its People, Vol. 1*, 450.
[14] *Acts of the Legislature of the State of Michigan, 1864*, 23.
[15] John M. Munson, *Michigan's White Pine Era, 1840-1900*, 34.
[16] *Cheboygan Daily Tribune, Golden Jubilee Edition*, 30 June 1939.
[17] *The Traverse Region*, 106-107.
[18] Maria Quinlan, "Lumbering in Michigan," *The Great Lakes Informant, Series 3, No. 2*, 3.
[19] *The Manitawauba Chronicle*, 6 May 1871.
[20] Ibid.
[21] Rodney C. Loehr, "Saving the Kerf: The Introduction of the Band Saw Mill," *Agricultural History* 23, No. 3 (July 1949): 169.
[22] *The Traverse Region*, 106-107.
[23] Ibid., 107.
[24] *Manitawauba Chronicle*, 25 March 1871.

[25] Gordon Turner, "Ghost Town Once Thrived Nearby," in *Pioneering North: Historical Highlights of the Cheboygan Area*, 9.

[26] I*nsurance Maps of Cheboygan, Michigan*, August 1890.

[27] Turner, "Ghost Town Once Thrived Nearby," 9.

[28] I*nsurance Maps of Cheboygan, Michigan*, August 1890.

[29] Ibid.; *Insurance Maps of Cheboygan, Michigan,* December 1895; *History of the Great Lakes, Illustrated, Vol. 1*, 818.

[30] Gerald F. Micketti, in correspondence with the author; Ellis Olson, *Cheboygan Historical Sketches* (Cheboygan, MI: Cheboygan Area Chamber of Commerce, 1976), 44.

[31] Ellis N. Olson, "Historical Development of River," 31.

[32] Ibid., 33.

[33] "Cheboygan County," *The Traverse Region,* 111; mail survey

[34] Ellis N. Olson, "Historical Development of River," 33.

[35] Marciana, *Serving You*, 174.

[36] Ware, *The Centennial History,* 26. Interestingly, even as late as 1884 the area immediately east of the Cheboygan River was often referred to as "West Duncan," implying that the greater settlement was Duncan City and not Cheboygan. Despite this, the momentum was clearly in favor of the latter, and by 1890 West Duncan had fallen into disuse in favor of the more sensical, broader (and official) name of Cheboygan.

[37] Robinson, *History of Cheboygan and Mackinaw Counties*, 22, 44.

[38] Fosimire, "History of Cheboygan," 6-7. For an explanation of this technicality, see Appendix B.

[39] Ware, *The Centennial History,* 26.

[40] Ellis Olson, *Wood Butchers of the North*, 26.

3. The Boom Begins

[1] *Cheboygan Daily Tribune, Golden Jubilee Edition*, 30 June 1939; Ellis Olson, in conversation with the author, 5 November 2005.

[2] *Official Railroad Map of the State of Michigan, 1901.*

[3] This list of settlements was compiled from the *Official Railroad Map of the State of Michigan, 1901,* and Lawton T. Hemans, *Official Railroad Map of the State of Michigan Showing Steam and Electric Lines, September 1913.*

[4] *Cheboygan Daily Tribune, Golden Jubilee Edition*, 30 June 1939.

[5] This list of settlements was compiled from A.J. Farmer, *Official Railroad Map of the State of Michigan, 1906-1907* and Lawton T. Hemans, *Official Railroad Map of the State of Michigan Showing Steam and Electric Lines, September1913.*

[5] *Cheboygan Daily Tribune, Golden Jubilee Edition*, 30 June 1939.

[6] Carl Bajema, "Timber Express," *Michigan History Magazine,* November / December 1993, 42-44.

[7] Ibid., 46, 42.

[8] *Northern Tribune,* 23 February 1878

[9] Forrest B. Meek, *Logging Railroads of Michigan, 1870-1886,* 31, 48.

[10] The following year, a water system was installed on the east side of the river, at a cost of $6,125.42. *Cheboygan Daily Tribune, Golden Jubilee Edition,* 30 June 1939.

[11] Ibid.

[12] Ibid.; Ellis Olson, in conversation with the author, 5 November 2005. The cement used in paving the downtown was a gift of M.D. Olds.

[13] Robinson, *History of Cheboygan and Mackinaw Counties,* 42-43, and rear advertising section.

[14] Ware, *The Centennial History,* 17-19.

[15] *Cheboygan Daily Tribune, Golden Jubilee Edition,* 30 June 1939.

[16] An article discussing lynching in Michigan was published in the Spring 2005 *Chronicles* of the Historical Society of Michigan. The article describes Till Warner as African-American, though there is no evidence to support this.

[17] *The Northern Tribune,* 16 June 1883.

[18] Ibid.; *The Detroit Free Press,* 14 June 1883.

[19] *The Northern Tribune,* 16 June 1883.

[20] Ibid.; *The Detroit Free Press,* 15 June 1883.

[21] *The Northern Tribune,* 16 June 1883.

[22] Ibid.

[23] Ibid.

[24] Both quotes taken from *The Northern Tribune,* 23 June 1883.

[25] *The Detroit Free Press,* 16 June 1883.

[26] Ibid.

[27] *Cheboygan Daily Tribune, Golden Jubilee Edition,* 30 June 1939; *The Traverse Region,* 108.

[28] *Northern Tribune,* 14 January 1882; 11 February 1882.

[29] T.H. Hinchman, *Banks and Banking in Michigan,* 150; Powers, *A History of Northern Michigan and its People, Vol. 1,* 456-457.

[30] Hinchman, *Banks and Banking in Michigan,* 150, and Emory Wendell, *History of Banks and Banking in Michigan, Vol. 2,* 319.

[31] Hinchman, *Banks and Banking in Michigan,* 66; Powers, *A History of Northern Michigan and its People, Vol. 1,* 457.

[32] *Cheboygan Daily Tribune, Golden Jubilee Edition,* 30 June 1939.

[33] Ibid.

[34] D.L. Gibson, *Socio-Economic Evolution in a Timbered Area in Northern Michigan,* 6.

[35] Robinson, *History of Cheboygan and Mackinaw Counties,* 24.

[36] *Local Acts of the Legislature of the State of Michigan, 1889,* 269-365.

4. Unprecedented Prosperity

[1] *Insurance Maps of Cheboygan, Michigan,* August 1890.

[2] Ibid.

3 *Cheboygan Daily Tribune, Golden Jubilee Edition,* 30 June 1939.

4 Ibid.

5 *Cheboygan Daily Tribune, Golden Jubilee Edition,* 30 June 1939.

6 Gibson, *Socio-Economic Evolution in a Timbered Area in Northern Michigan,* 13-14.

7 *Insurance Maps of Cheboygan, Michigan,* December 1895.

8 Atwood, "Cheboygan as a Nineteenth Century Lumber Area," 58-59.

9 Promotional *Pocket Map of Michigan and Wisconsin, presented with the compliments of W. & A. McArthur Company, Ltd,* private collection.

10 *Cheboygan Daily Tribune, Golden Jubilee Edition,* 30 June 1939.

11 Atwood, "Cheboygan as a Nineteenth Century Lumber Area," 63.

12 *Insurance Maps of Cheboygan, Michigan,* December 1895.

13 Promotional *Pocket Map of Michigan and Wisconsin, presented with the compliments of W. & A. McArthur Company, Ltd.*

14 Atwood, "Cheboygan as a Nineteenth Century Lumber Area," 65-66.

15 Ibid., 62. Atwood states that McArthur's yard was the first in Cheboygan, that "there were no retail lumber yards before that time." I question this statement, however, as there was rapid growth in Cheboygan and Duncan City that could not have been possible without freely available lumber, of which there was clearly no shortage. Regardless, it was unquestionably among the first.

16 *Cheboygan Democrat,* 15 and 8 December 1894.

17 *Cheboygan Daily Tribune, Golden Jubilee Edition,* 30 June 1939.

18 Promotional *Pocket Map of Michigan and Wisconsin, presented with the compliments of W. & A. McArthur Company, Ltd.*

19 *Cheboygan Daily Tribune, Golden Jubilee Edition,* 30 June 1939.

20 Gibson, *Socio-Economic Evolution in a Timbered Area in Northern Michigan,* 12.

21 Ibid., 7, 9.

22 Ibid., 24.

23 Edward Forsyth, "Cheboygan County," in *Michigan and its Resources,* Michigan Department of State, 221.

24 This was probably the peak of Cheboygan's population. The census returns of 1894 show the city population at 6957; by the time of the federal census in 1900 it was down to 6489. It is conceivable that the population was at one time higher between these two dates, but there is no way to confirm this. Ellis N. Olson, "Population Census of Cheboygan," *Cheboygan Centennial 1889-1989,* 33.

25 Benson, *Logs and Lumber,* 197.

26 University of Virginia, *Geostat Center: Historical Census Browser,* "Michigan, Cheboygan County," http://fisher.lib.virginia.edu/collections/stats/histcensus/ (accessed 20 November 2004).

27 Olson, *Wood Butchers of the North,* 26.

28 James Elliot Defebaugh, *History of the Lumber Industry in America, Vol. 1,* 445-6.

29 Ibid., 445-58.

30 Ibid., 457-9.

31 *The Cheboygan News,* 10 October 1900; *Insurance Maps of Cheboygan, Michigan,* October 1900.

32 *Cheboygan Democrat,* 1 October 1898.

33 Ibid.

34 *Cheboygan Daily Tribune,* 29 September 1898, qtd. in *Cheboygan Daily Tribune, Golden Jubilee Edition,* 30 June 1939.

35 *Cheboygan Democrat,* 1 October 1898.

36 Gordon Turner, "Ghost Town Once Thrived Nearby," 9.

37 Olson, *Cheboygan Historical Sketches,* 47.

38 Olson, "When Lumber Was King," 46. Interestingly, although Duncan did rapidly depopulate at the turn of the century, it was still shown as a separate settlement on the United States War Department's *Chart of Island Route of Navigation - Michigan* as late as February, 1916.

39 *Cheboygan Democrat,* 1 November 1888.

40 *Cheboygan, Up-to-Date,* qtd. in Forsyth, "Cheboygan County," in *Michigan and its Resources,* 221.

41 Fosimire, "History of Cheboygan," 12.

42 *Insurance Maps of Cheboygan, Michigan,* October 1900 and August 1907.

43 Fosimire, "History of Cheboygan," 12.

44 Olson, *Wood Butchers of the North,* 32.

45 Atwood, "Cheboygan as a Nineteenth Century Lumber Area," 127.

46 *Cheboygan Democrat,* 15 October 1891.

47 Atwood, "Cheboygan as a Nineteenth Century Lumber Area," 125-126.

48 Ibid.

49 Powers, *A History of Northern Michigan and its People, Vol. 1,* 456.

50 *Cheboygan Democrat,* 24 March 1894.

51 Mary L. Gunther, in discussion with the author, May 2005; *Insurance Maps of Cheboygan, Michigan,* September 1915 and September 1923.

52 *Cheboygan Democrat,* 8 September 1900.

53 *Cheboygan Democrat,* 7 July 1900.

54 The brothers owned two boats and had three stores and a share in a bottling plant in Au Sable, Michigan. *The Northern Tribune,* 26 May 1883; Olson, *Cheboygan Historical Sketches,* 26; "Cheboygan County," *The Traverse Region,* 109.

55 *Cheboygan Daily Tribune, Golden Jubilee Edition,* 30 June 1939.

56 Atwood, "Cheboygan as a Nineteenth Century Lumber Area," 128.

57 Gordon Turner, "Of the Days When We Were a Fishing Town," in *Pioneering North: Historical Highlights of the Cheboygan Area,* 17.

58 Powers, *A History of Northern Michigan and its People, Vol. 1,* 456.

59 Gordon Turner, "Cheboygan Snowplows Made Way For Sleighs," in *Pioneering North: Historical Highlights of the Cheboygan Area,* 37.

60 P.B. Brazel to E.A. Brazel, 22 July 1909, private collection; Gordon Turner, "Cheboygan Snowplows Made Way For Sleighs," 37.

61 Beverly Rae Kimes, *Standard Catalog of American Cars, 1805-1942* (Iola, WI: Krause Publications, Inc, 1985), 518; Ellis Olson, in conversation with the author, 5 November 2005.

62 Kimes, *Standard Catalog of American Cars,* 518.

63 Ellis Olson, in conversation with the author, 5 November 2005.

[64] *Cheboygan Daily Tribune, Golden Jubilee Edition,* 30 June 1939; University of Virginia, *Geostat Center: Historical Census Browser,* "Michigan, Cheboygan County," http://fisher.lib.virginia.edu/collections/stats/histcensus/php/county.php (accessed 10 August 2005).
[65] *Cheboygan Daily Tribune, Golden Jubilee Edition,* 30 June 1939.

5. Of Shanty Boys and Lumber Barons

[1] Ellis Olson, in conversation with the author, 5 November 2005.
[2] *Cheboygan Observer,* 12 September 1935; M.D. Olds papers, Clarke Historical Library, Central Michigan University. The former source indicates Olds' partner was named Hinkley, but this is not correct. The evidence shows that the partnership which Olds bought into was subsequently called "Olds & Hixson," according to contemporary letterheads from that business.
[3] *Cheboygan Daily Tribune,* 9 September 1935. Interestingly, as early as April 1903 Olds' logmark "HJ" was being used in the Cheboygan river. The amount of his logs passing through the Cheboygan River Boom Company was not particularly large, but nor were they by any means negligible. Thus, from fairly early on Olds was doing a considerable business, even in the interim period after the fire at his stave mill in 1897 and the acquisition of Nelson & Clark seven years later. See W.W. Hornell, "Journal of the Cheboygan River Boom Co." M.D. Olds papers, Clarke Historical Library, Central Michigan University, 22-24.
[4] Ellis Olson, in conversation with the author, 5 November 2005; Ellis Olson, *Wood Butchers of the North,* 27, 31.
[5] Ibid., 32.
[6] *Insurance Maps of Cheboygan, Michigan,* August 1907.
[7] M.D. Olds to Bartlett Lumber Company, 24 and 26 August 1916. Olds elaborated, saying, "We have two Prescott bands, one 9 ft. and one 10 ft., both carriages are equipped with steam feed and steam set. We have one resaw with a Mershon feed works of large size. It is a 9 ft. Prescott band mill that we have it attached to. It is a fine working machine and never has given us a minutes [sic] trouble since we put it in the mill."
[8] *Insurance Maps of Cheboygan, Michigan,* August 1907; Powers, *A History of Northern Michigan and its People, Vol. 1,* 456.
[9] Powers, *A History of Northern Michigan and its People, Vol. 1,* 456.
[10] This is probably a reference to "Duck Marsh", located in the southeast corner of this particular section (T-37-N, R-1-E, Sec. 8). M.D. Olds papers, Clarke Historical Library, Central Michigan University.
[11] Theodore J. Karamanski, *Deep Woods Frontier: A History of Logging in Northern Michigan,* 67.
[12] Atwood, "Cheboygan as a Nineteenth Century Lumber Area," 13-14; Lawrence Boucha, interview by University of Wisconsin graduate students, 12 August 1982.

[13] Lawrence Boucha, interview by University of Wisconsin graduate students, 12 August 1982, private collection.

[14] Ibid.

[15] Atwood, "Cheboygan as a Nineteenth Century Lumber Area," 13-14; Ellis Olson, in conversation with the author, 5 November 2005.

[16] Lawrence Boucha, interview by University of Wisconsin graduate students, 12 August 1982.

[17] Benson, *Logs and Lumber,* 80.

[18] M.D. Olds papers, Clarke Historical Library, Central Michigan University; Olds Family Website: www.olds-family.com/jerhur.html. 17 April 2005.

[19] Benson, *Logs and Lumber,* 152.

[20] W.W. Hornell, "Journal of the Cheboygan River Boom Co." M.D. Olds papers, Clarke Historical Library, Central Michigan University.

[21] Olds Family website: www.olds-family.com/milold.html. 17 April 2005.

[22] Ellis Olson, in conversation with the author, 5 November 2005.

[23] Ibid.

[24] M.D. Olds papers, Clarke Historical Library, Central Michigan University.

[25] Lloyd M. Atwood, "Cheboygan as a Nineteenth Century Lumber Area," 18-19.

[26] Collection register for Mrs. Lewis Wright, M.D. Olds papers, Clarke Historical Library, Central Michigan University.

[27] M.D. Olds papers, Clarke Historical Library, Central Michigan University.

[28] *Manitawauba Chronicle,* 11 March 1871.

[29] *Daily Engine Room Reports,* M.D. Olds papers, Clarke Historical Library, Central Michigan University.

[30] *The Northern Tribune,* 15 September 1883.

[31] M.D. Olds papers, Clarke Historical Library, Central Michigan University.

[32] Ibid.

[33] Ibid.

[34] Ibid.

[35] Olds to Mrs. G. T. Chamberlain, 31 October 1911. M.D. Olds, Papers, Clarke Historical Library, Central Michigan University.

[36] Olds to Miss Florence Olds, 30 October 1908. M.D. Olds, Papers, Clarke Historical Library, Central Michigan University.

[37] Ibid.

[38] Ibid.

[39] *Cheboygan Daily Tribune, Golden Jubilee Edition,* 30 June 1939.

[40] Olds to Miss Florence Olds, 30 October 1908. M.D. Olds, Papers, Clarke Historical Library, Central Michigan University.

[41] Gerald Micketti, *The Day Metz Burned,* 15.

[42] M.D. Olds to A.W. Layman (U.S. General Land Office), 1 March 1909, M.D. Olds papers, Clarke Historical Library, Central Michigan University.

[43] Correspondence with various lumber companies. M.D. Olds papers, Clarke Historical Library, Central Michigan University.

[44] Pfister & Vogel Leather Co. to M.D. Olds, 4 May 1909, and reply, 15 May 1909, M.D. Olds papers, Clarke Historical Library, Central Michigan University.

[45] Olson, "Historical Development of River," 32.
[46] Olson, *Wood Butchers of the North,* 30-32.
[47] Olds to Mrs. G. T. Chamberlain, 31 October 1911. M.D. Olds papers, Clarke Historical Library, Central Michigan University.
[48] M.D. Olds papers, Clarke Historical Library, Central Michigan University.

6. Winds of Change

[1] D.L. Gibson, *Socio-Economic Evolution in a Timbered Area in Northern Michigan,* 30.
[2] Fosimire, "History of Cheboygan," 13.
[3] M.D. Olds to Bartlett Lumber Company, 16 August 1916.
[4] *Insurance Maps of Cheboygan, Michigan,* September 1915.
[5] *Cheboygan Democrat,* 9 March 1922; Ellis Olson, in conversation with the author, 5 November 2005.
[6] Ibid.
[7] *Cheboygan Democrat,* 9 March 1922.
[8] Ibid.
[9] Ibid.
[10] *To Commemorate 100 Years of Service: Pfister and Vogel Tanning Company* (Milwaukee: Pfister and Vogel Tanning Company [?], 1948), 11.
[11] *Cheboygan Observer,* 2 February 1950.
[12] *Cheboygan Observer,* 22 November 1928. Note that this is not the modern Cheboygan State Park, but rather that which existed at the corner of Lincoln and Garfield Avenues.
[13] *Insurance Maps of Cheboygan, Michigan,* August 1907.
[14] *Cheboygan Daily Tribune,* 15 November 1928 and *Cheboygan Observer,* 22 November 1928.
[15] Ibid.
[16] *Cheboygan Daily Tribune,* 11 June 1930.
[17] Ibid.
[18] Unknown writer to Millard D. Olds, 15 June 1930. M.D. Olds papers, Clarke Historical Library, Central Michigan University.
[19] Ibid., 74.
[20] *Cheboygan Daily Tribune,* 9 September 1935; M.D. Olds papers, Clarke Historical Library, Central Michigan University.
[21] University of Virginia, *Geostat Center: Historical Census Browser,* "Michigan, Cheboygan County," http://fisher.lib.virginia.edu/collections/stats/histcensus/ (accessed 26 August 2005).
[22] Titus, "Cheboygan's Chin is Up," 73.

7. Remnants of a Bygone Era

[1] *Cheboygan Daily Tribune,* 15 November 1928.

[2] Gordon Turner, "Sawmill Ruins Recall an Era," in *Pioneering North: Historical Highlights of the Cheboygan Era,* 12.

[3] http://www.theoperahouse.org/. Accessed 11 September 2005.

[4] Gordon Turner, "In Search of the Hidden Locomotive," in *Pioneering North: Historical Highlights of the Cheboygan Era,* 12.

[5] Karamanski, *Deep Woods Frontier,* 174.

[6] Ibid.

[7] M.D. Olds papers, Clarke Historical Library, Central Michigan University.

[8] In a letter dated 26 April 1920, M.D. Olds writes to his daughter Gertrude that he and his wife "went to the hotel for dinner yesterday. The Martins, the Boggs, Hugills, Shephards, Dr. Chapman and his son, were also there." The Martins are probably those of the Embury-Martin Lumber Company. What is more, Harris Embury and members of his family are buried almost next to Olds. See M.D. Olds papers, Clarke Historical Library, Central Michigan University.

[9] Willard Baird, *This is Our Michigan* (Battle Creek, MI: Federated Publications, Inc., 1954), 28.

[10] Cf. C.B. Headley, "The Pine Forests of Michigan," *The Lumberman's Gazette,* July 1872, 4.

For Further Reading

Local history often presents a particular challenge in that, because of its limited scope, it can be exceedingly difficult to find additional information about the particular region or topic being studied. Additionally, some of those sources can be exceptionally challenging to locate, especially if they were published many decades ago or were not formally published at all. The bibliography at the end of this book lists all the sources I have cited, but here I wish to point the reader to some more easily accessible and engaging material which will enhance one's understanding of Cheboygan and the lumber industry in northern Michigan.

The first book compiled specifically about Cheboygan is Rev. W.H. Ware's *Centennial History of Cheboygan County and Village* (Cheboygan, MI: Northern Tribune Printing, 1876). Entertaining and informative, it lists not only just about every local "first" imaginable, but also lists businesses, stores, and shops and their proprietors. Reprinted editions by the Historical Society of Cheboygan County in 1976 and 1996 make this book readily available.

A more scholarly work assembled on Cheboygan is Lloyd M. Atwood's "Cheboygan as a Nineteenth Century Lumber Area" (Master's thesis, Wayne University, 1947). While not formally published, the accuracy and depth of this study is remarkable, and anyone wishing to know more about the birth of Cheboygan as a lumbering community must consult it. The economic aspects of the region's lumber industry are brilliantly discussed in D.L. Gibson's *Socio-Economic Evolution in a Timbered Area in Northern Michigan* (East Lansing, MI: Michigan State College, 1944). Gibson's analysis of exactly how lumber caused the rise and fall of Cheboygan's economy is discussed with an unprecedented clarity and readability, not to mention the historical facts that are consequently discussed.

Anyone interested in Cheboygan history owes a debt of gratitude to Ellis Olson, without whom a great deal of information about the community's early days would have been lost. Most notably relevant to the study of lumber is *Wood Butchers of the North* (Cheboygan, MI: Cheboygan Daily Tribune, 1971). This book is engaging, fun to read, and full of essential knowledge. What sets this book apart from all others is the compiled list of Cheboygan County logmarks, as well as a listing of nearly every mill or operator who ever conducted business in Cheboygan, along with the dates of operation. An additional comprehensive history can be found in Olson's *Cheboygan Historical Sketches* (Cheboygan, MI: Cheboygan Area Chamber of Commerce, 1976, 1979), complete with an excellent and meticulous chronicle of not only Cheboygan but Duncan City as well. Additional work by Olson can be found in *Cheboygan Centennial 1871-1971: 100 Years on the Straits* and *Cheboygan Centennial 1889-1989* (Cheboygan, MI: City of Cheboygan, 1971, 1989 respectively). All of Olson's compilations can be found at the Cheboygan County Historical Society's Museum, most of which are available for purchase. Reprints of Ware's *Centennial History of Cheboygan County and Village* are also available.

Cheboygan's various newspapers which have operated off and on for the past 135 or so years are, of course, an endless source of information. They are fascinating, relatively easy to locate on microfilm, and provide the inquisitive historian or genealogist with more material then he or she could possibly ever sort through. I would advise that one concentrate on key dates and periods, especially those dates which I have mentioned in the chronology or those that appear throughout the text. The columns by "Mr. Cheboygan," Gordon Turner, are of special mention. In his sixty years of writing for the *Cheboygan Daily Tribune*, Turner acquired enough knowledge about the history of his town to fill the pages of the newspaper for several lifetimes. His weekly columns talked about a wide range of topics, many of which dealt specifically with Cheboygan's early history. The most popular of these columns were published in a book entitled *Pioneering North: Historical Highlights of the Cheboygan Area* (Cheboygan, MI: Cheboygan Daily Tribune, 1987). For the historian or casual reader, Turner's work cannot be neglected.

Lastly, if a more general history of lumbering in Michigan is of interest, there are several excellent books available. Barbara Benson's *Logs and Lumber: The Development of Lumbering in Michigan's Lower Peninsula,*

1837-1870 (Mt. Pleasant, MI: Clarke Historical Library, 1989) is considered a pivotal work on the industry in Michigan. It examines various aspects of lumbering in a very thorough and complete analysis. Theodore J. Karamanski's *Deep Woods Frontier: A History of Logging in Northern Michigan* (Detroit: Wayne State University Press, 1989) examines many of the same issues, but concentrates primarily on the Upper Peninsula. A comparative analysis of three larger lumber towns can be found in Jeremy W. Kilar's *Michigan's Lumbertowns: Lumbermen and Laborers in Saginaw, Bay City and Muskegon, 1870-1905*. Colorful stories and first-rate research make this book a profoundly valuable analysis of how differently (and similarly) a new industry can influence communities.

If Cheboygan County and / or Michigan history interests you, it is worthwhile to consider membership in these organizations:

Historical Society of Cheboygan County, Inc.
P.O. Box 5005
Cheboygan, MI 49721
www.cheboyganmuseum.com

Mackinac Associates
P.O. Box 567
Mackinaw City, MI 49701-0567
http://www.mackinacparks.com/parks/mackinac-associates

The Historical Society of Michigan
1305 Abbott Rd.
East Lansing, MI 48823
www.hsmichigan.org

Our heritage will only be preserved if we are willing to step up to the challenge and take an active role in preserving that legacy. Get involved!

Bibliography

BOOKS, ARTICLES, NEWSPAPERS, AND MANUSCRIPT COLLECTIONS

Acts of the Legislature of the State of Michigan: 1840. Detroit: George Dawson, State Printer, 1840.

Acts of the Legislature of the State of Michigan: 1849. Lansing, MI: Munger and Pattison, Printers to the State, 1849.

Acts of the Legislature of the State of Michigan: 1853. Lansing, MI: George W. Peck, Printer to the State, 1853.

Acts of the Legislature of the State of Michigan: 1861. Lansing, MI: John A. Kerr and Company, Printers to the State, 1861.

Acts of the Legislature of the State of Michigan: 1864. Lansing, MI: John A. Kerr and Company, Printers to the State, 1864.

Acts of the Legislature of the State of Michigan: 1869. Lansing, MI: W.S. George and Company, Printers to the State, 1869.

Acts of the Legislature of the State of Michigan: 1871, Vol. 2, 3. Lansing, MI: W.S. George & Co., Printers to the State, 1871.

Atwood, Lloyd M. "Cheboygan as a Nineteenth Century Lumber Area." Master's thesis, Wayne University, 1947.

Baird, Willard. *This is Our Michigan*. Battle Creek, MI: Federated Publications, Inc., 1954.

Bajema, Carl. "Timber Express." *Michigan History Magazine*. November / December 1993, 42-46.

Benson, Barbara E. *Logs and Lumber: The Development of Lumbering in Michigan's Lower Peninsula, 1837-1870*. Mt. Pleasant, MI: Clarke Historical Library, 1989.

Cheboygan Daily Tribune. 15 November 1928.

———. 11 June 1930.

———. 9 September 1935.

———. Golden Jubilee Edition, 30 June 1939.

Cheboygan Democrat. 1 November 1888.

———. 15 October 1891.

———. 24 March 1894.

———. 1 January 1897.

———. 8 December 1897.

———. 15 December 1897.

———. 7 July 1900.

———. 8 September 1900.

———. 9 March 1922.

Cheboygan News, The. 10 October 1900.

Cheboygan Observer. 22 November 1928.

———. 12 September 1935.

———. 2 February 1950.

Cheboygan Opera House, The. http://www.theoperahouse.org/.

Defebaugh, James Elliot. *History of the Lumber Industry of America, Vol. 1.* Chicago: The American Lumberman, 1906.

Detroit Free Press, The. 14 June 1883.

———. 15 June 1883.

———. 16 June 1883.

Etulain, Richard W. *Does the Frontier Experience Make America Exceptional?* Boston: Bedford / St. Martin's, 1999.

Forsyth, Edward. "Cheboygan County," *Michigan and its Resources.* Michigan Department of State. Lansing, MI: Robert Smith & Co., 1893.

Fosimire, Michael. "History of Cheboygan," *When I Was Your Age: Students Look at Cheboygan History and the World Today.* Cheboygan, MI:Cheboygan Area High School, May 1971.

Fuller, George N., ed. Historic Michigan: *Land of the Great Lakes, Vol. 1.* National Historical Commission, 1924[?].

Gibson, D.L. *Michigan Technical Bulletin 193.* "Socio-Economic Evolution in a Timbered Area in Northern Michigan." East Lansing, MI: Michigan State College, 1944.

Grimm, Joe, ed. *Michigan Voices: Our State's History in the Words of the People Who Lived It.* Detroit: Detroit Free Press, 1987.

Hinchman, T.H. *Banks and Banking in Michigan.* Detroit: Wm. Graham, 1887.

History of the Great Lakes, Illustrated, Vol. 1. Chicago: J.H. Beers and Company, 1899.

Insurance Maps of Cheboygan, Michigan. Sanborn-Perris Map Co., Ltd., August 1890.

————. December 1895.

————. October 1900.

————. August 1907.

————. September 1915.

————. September 1923.

Karamanski, Theodore J. *Deep Woods Frontier: A History of Logging in Northern Michigan*. Detroit: Wayne State University Press, 1989.

Kimes, Beverly Rae. *Standard Catalog of American Cars, 1805-1942*. Iola, WI: Krause Publications, Inc, 1985.

"Land Patent Search." *Bureau of Land Management, General Land Office Records*. http://www.glorecords.blm.gov/.

Local Acts of the Legislature of the State of Michigan: 1877. Lansing, MI: W.S. George & Co., State Printers and Binders, 1877.

Loehr, Rodney C. "Saving the Kerf: The Introduction of the Band Saw Mill." *Agricultural History* 23, No. 3 (July 1949): 168-172.

Manitawauba Chronicle, The. 11 February 1871.

————. 11 March 1871.

————. 25 March 1871.

———— 6 May 1871.

Marciana, Sr., SSJ, ed. *Serving You: Post Offices of Michigan 1802-1976*. Hastings, MI: Hastings Commercial Printers, 1977.

Meek, Forrest B. *Logging Railroads of Michigan, 1870-1886*. Clare, MI: White Pine Historical Society, 1986.

Meyers, P.A and J.A. Meyers. *Plat Book of Cheboygan County, Michigan: Drawn from Actual Surveys and the County Records.* Minneapolis: Consolidated Publishing Company, 1902.

Michigan: Official Directory and Legislative Manual, 1929-1930. Lansing: State of Michigan, 1930.

Michigan Pioneer and Historical Collections, Vol. 9, 1886, 2nd ed. Lansing: Wynkoop Hallenbeck Crawford Company, State Printers, 1908.

Micketti, Gerald. *The Day Metz Burned.* Alpena, MI: Gerald Micketti, 1992.

Munson, John M. *Michigan's White Pine Era, 1840-1900.* Lansing, MI: Michigan Historical Commission, 1964.

Northern Tribune, The. 17 July 1875.

————.23 February 1878.

————. 14 January 1882.

————. 11 February 1882.

————. 26 May 1883.

————. 16 June 1883.

————. 23 June 1883.

————. 15 September 1883.

————. 11 December 1884.

Olds Family website: www.olds-family.com/milold.html.

Olds, Millard David. Papers. Clarke Historical Library, Central Michigan University.

Olson, Ellis. Papers. Private collection.

———. *Cheboygan Historical Sketches*. Cheboygan, MI: Cheboygan Area Chamber of Commerce, 1976, 1979.

———. "Historical Development of River," *Cheboygan Centennial 1889-1989*. Cheboygan, MI: City of Cheboygan, 1989.

———. "When Lumber was King," *Cheboygan Centennial 1871-1971: 100 Years on the Straits*. Cheboygan, MI: City of Cheboygan (?), 1971.

———. *Wood Butchers of the North*. Cheboygan, MI: Cheboygan Daily Tribune, 1971.

Powers, Perry F. *A History of Northern Michigan and its People, Vol. 1*. Chicago: The Lewis Publishing Company, 1912.

Quaife, Milo M., ed. *The John Askin Papers*. Detroit: Detroit Library Commission, 1928.

Quinlan, Maria. "Lumbering in Michigan." Lansing, MI [?]: *The Great Lakes Informant, Series 3, No. 2*. Michigan Department of State, Michigan History Division, 1986.

Romig, Walter. *Michigan Place Names*. Grosse Pointe, MI: Walter Romig, Publisher, 1973[?]

Robinson, George and R.A. Sprague. *History of Cheboygan and Mackinaw Counties*. Detroit: Union Job Printing Company, 1873.

Rubenstein, Bruce A. and Lawrence E. Ziewacz. *Michigan: A History of the Great Lakes State*, 3rd ed. Wheeling, IL: Harlan Davidson, 2002.

Scharf, J. Thomas. *History of Delaware, 1609-1888, Vol. II*. Philadelphia: L.J. Richards & Co., 1888.

"Statewide Search for Subdivision Plats." *Michigan Department of Labor and Economic Growth, Bureau of Construction Codes and Fire Safety.* http://www.cis.state.mi.us/.

Steer, Henry B. See United States Department of Agriculture.

Stempky, Carol. *The History of the Catholic Church "St. Mary's," Cheboygan, Michigan.* Cheboygan, MI: Carol Stempky, 1998.

Titus, Harold. "Cheboygan's Chin is Up." *The Saturday Evening Post*, 6 July 1946.

To Commemorate 100 Years of Service: Pfister and Vogel Tanning Company. Milwaukee: Pfister and Vogel Tanning Company [?], 1948.

Traverse Region, Historical and Descriptive, Illustrated, The. Chicago: H.R. Page and Co., 1884.

Turner, Gordon. *Pioneering North: Historical Highlights of the Cheboygan Area.* Cheboygan, MI: Cheboygan Daily Tribune, 1987.

United States. Light-House Board. *List of Light-Houses, Lighted Beacons, and Floating Lights of the United States.* Washington: William A. Harris, 1858.

United States Department of Agriculture. *Lumber Production in the United States, 1799-1946. United States Department of Agriculture Miscellaneous Publication No. 669*, by Henry B. Steer. Washington, DC: U.S. Government Printing Office, 1948.

University of Virginia, Geostat Center: Historical Census Browser, "Michigan, Cheboygan County," http://fisher.lib.virginia.edu/collections/stats/histcensus/php/county.php.

Ware, W.H., Rev. *Centennial History of Cheboygan County and Village, The.* Cheboygan, MI: Northern Tribune Printing, 1876.

MAPS

Cheboygan County, Michigan. Cincinnati: Hampton Publishing Company, 2005[?].

Hemans, Lawton T. *Official Railroad Map Showing Steam and Electric Lines of the State of Michigan, September 1913*. Buffalo, NY: The Matthews – Northrup Works, 1913.

Official Railroad Map of the State of Michigan, 1901. Milwaukee: Northwestern Lithograph Company, 1901.

Pocket Map of Michigan and Wisconsin, Presented with the Compliments of W. & A. McArthur Co., Ltd. Chicago: The Jno. F. Waite Publishing Company, Engravers and Printers, 1895[?].

Index

ISBN 141208304-4